TEACHING TO THE HEART

An Affective Approach
to Literacy Instruction
Second Edition

Nancy Lee Cecil

California State University, Sacramento

Sheffield Publishing Company

Salem, Wisconsin

For information about this book, write or call:
    Sheffield Publishing Company
    P.O. Box 359
    Salem, Wisconsin 53168
    (414) 843-2281

Cover art by Susan Nace

Printed in the United States of America

7 6 5 4 3

TEACHING TO THE HEART:

An Affective Approach to Literacy Instruction, 2/E

Contents

TEACHING TO THE HEART:

An Affective Approach to Literacy Instruction, 2/E

Anecdotal Outline

Introduction. Establishes a need for an Affective Reading Program that creates children who *like* to read, rather than ones who *can* read, but don't.

1. **Setting Up An Affective Reading Program:** Describes the structure and management of the program and proposes various grouping arrangements.

2. **Creating a Positive Classroom Climate:** A healthy learning environment most conducive to reading, exploring, and critical thinking is the concern here. Sharing of progress and the enhancement of the self-concept through positive teacher behaviors is explored.

3. **Providing for Skill Development and Evaluation:** Explains the basics of teaching reading in such a way that skills are developed as they are needed rather than having time spent on useless drills. The importance of continual evaluation is highlighted.

4. **Emergent Literacy and the Language Experience:** Documents the importance of using children's vocabulary and interests to make the initial impressions of reading positive and meaningful. Details the approach to teaching LEA in a unique, "no-fail" way.

5. **Getting Meaning from the Printed Page:** Includes many techniques to make critical reading and thinking an integral part of the total reading program.

6. **Reading and Writing Poetry:** Provides an exciting structure and "formulas" to help make poetry possible and fun for children. Presents poetry as an ideal way for children to express their feelings and become open to reading about the feelings of others.

7. **Reading Through Creative Drama:** Outlines how to turn the natural playfulness of children into a desire to create skits, read plays, and finally create their own dramatic enterprises.

8. **The Incredible Instructional Cloze:** Describes an approach to reading instruction that increases students' comprehension while allowing them to experience the richness and variety of our language.

9. **Reading Aloud to Children:** Stresses the necessity of reading aloud to children at all grade levels, as often as possible, using a variety of techniques and materials. Explains "how to" and provides novel reading aloud ideas.

10. **The Total Teaching Triangle: Engaging the Parent:** Discusses the importance of good home-school communication and how to achieve it. Provides specific suggestions to give those parents who wish to work directly with their children, and more general guidelines for parents who want to help their child but aren't comfortable with home teaching.

11. **Creating Classroom Authors:** This chapter discusses how to inspire children to write down their innermost thoughts in an inviting writing center. Assisting the editing process, through student/teacher conferences, will also be described, as well as using the promise of "publication" as additional motivation.

12. **Reaching Culturally and Linguistically Diverse Learners:** More than ever an Affective Reading Program is needed to offer a nurturing environment in which ALL children can learn to read, write, and take risks. This chapter offers specific suggestions for the monolingual teacher who faces the challenge of culturally and linguistically diverse learners.

For Gary, with love

Preface

The second edition of *Teaching To The Heart,* like the previous edition, is designed to give teachers and preservice teachers suggestions about teaching literacy that are first directed to the heart—not the head—of learners. This affective approach to literacy instruction is based upon the belief that much more is gained, ultimately, by developing readers who choose to read than by creating readers who can read, but who do not.

The first edition was ahead of its time. When I spoke to colleagues about a classroom that was child-centered, where those children could choose from among many quality children's books, I initially met with much skepticism. No teacher would feel confident enough to de-emphasize, let alone discard, the almighty basal reader, I was warned. Since that time, there have been significant developments in the field of literacy instruction. Literature-based instruction is an idea whose time has finally come! The purpose of this second edition, therefore, is to provide an understanding of the current maze of ideas, concepts, and philosophies germane to a truly whole language classroom where real books are utilized to introduce children to the joys of reading.

Additionally, the second edition includes a discrete chapter on the specific needs of culturally and linguistically diverse learners. Although the text has been designed with the entire spectrum of learners in mind, I have found that teachers are searching for tools for the children with special needs that they are now finding in their classes in increasingly large numbers.

This new edition also contains updated information on authentic assessment of literacy and new ideas about teaching writing as a process. Further, all instructional suggestions have been revised with accessibility to linguistically diverse learners in mind.

All of the ideas in this book have been tried and proven successful through my own experience in inservice education and teacher education. The reader should remember, however, that what works well with one child may not be appropriate with another; similarly, ideas that are suitable for one grade level may not be suitable for another.

Finally, I wish to express my heartfelt gratitude to all the exceptional affective teachers who have provided opportunities for consultation, inservice, and workshops; the preservice students who enthusiastically tried out ideas; and the children who provided the ultimate evaluations. This book would not have been possible without them. Above all, I hope that you, the teachers of the future, will have equally joyful teaching experiences as you bring to life, in your own ways, the ideas outlined in this text.

And now here is my secret, a very simple secret:
It is only with the heart that one can see rightly;
What is essential is invisible to the eye.
      —Antoine de Saint-Exupery, *The Little Prince*

Introduction

As the "Great Debate" rambles on, fueled by the emergence of a disturbing booklet called "Becoming A Nation of Readers," many educators are taking a closer look at teachers, programs and practices, and the teaching of reading is being particularly scrutinized. While the validity of reportedly waning scores and the deterioration in skill development are controversial and questionable, some alarming statistics should be cause for concern: one sobering survey concluded that, on the average, high school graduates read fewer than two books per year, while college graduates read less than three (Smith, 1980)! How can these statistics be reconciled with the fact that in the elementary school years children sit through more than 2,000 hours of reading instruction?

Since the era of the early McGuffey readers, the improvement in the style, content, illustrations, and general appeal of the modern basal reader, which is the most common tool used for instruction in reading, has been appreciable. Consider this rather morbid excerpt from a reader of the 1800s:

> Who loves a horse race? Are not too many fond of it? Does it not lead to many evils, and to frequent ruin? Never go to a horse race. Mr. Mix had one child, whom he called Irene; he also had a good farm and some money. He went to the races with his child, dressed in black crepe for the loss of her mother. Here Mr. Mix drank freely, and bet largely, and lost all he was worth. At night he went home a beggar, took doses of brandy, and died before morning, leaving his child a penniless orphan. Never go to a horse race.
> —from Clifton Johnson's *Old Time Schools and School Books*

It seems astonishing, perhaps, that many children *did* learn to read back then, despite the dreary nature of the reading material that was presented to them! Yet there have always seemed to be children, now and then, for whom the act of reading has been a somewhat natural process—developmentally similar to learning to talk, while motivationally more in line with learning how to navigate a skateboard. At the heart of the issue seems to be the query, "How do we spark that enthusiasm and keen interest in reading for *all* children?"

Although reading selections presented to children today may be considered unassailably more interesting than those which Johnson uncovered in his 1800s reader, one wonders just how much progress has actually been made since that time in providing motivational material to young readers. While there are over 40,000 exciting children's books on the market today, are they managing to find their way into most elementary reading programs? In examining the current research on children's literature, one finds instead that the basal reader is used by at least 80 percent of U.S. elementary classroom teachers as the core—if not the sum total—of their reading programs (Pieronek, 1980). Yet no matter how greatly improved these readers have become, they are still not the books that children would most willingly read by choice (Busch, 1972; Meisel and Glass, 1970; Pieronek, 1980; Tibbetts, 1974).

The reasons for this relative unpopularity of basal readers are open to speculation. One common suggestion is that children quickly learn that the basal reader is not to be associated with "enjoyable reading," because it will inevitably be followed by tedious drills, questions, and extended activity assignments. Another equally valid observation might be that students are generally put into skill groups for basal reading instruction. They are then compelled to all read the same story at the same allotted time. When we consider our own recreational reading habits, don't we find that our interest fluctuates for a hundred different reasons? Don't we require an extensive "background" in a subject before we can thoroughly enjoy it? Don't we usually have to be "in the mood" to read? And moreover, don't we truly cherish our rights as individuals to select the exact book that we would most like to read?

To illustrate these points, I often ask my classes of preservice teachers, who all emphatically declare that they are "avid readers," to read the following paragraph:

> As suggested by Thomas, all allocation methods must be based upon some concept of a distribution of benefits expected to be received by using an asset over time (its net revenue contribution each period) or else the allocation must be arbitrary and thus meaningless as a measure of a rational concept of income. However, Thomas also suggests from his research study that rarely would it be possible to measure either the *ex ante* or *ex post* net revenue contributions in the several periods during the use of an asset, because of the many interactions of the production functions or inputs in the production and other operating processes of a firm. Three possible alternatives to this dilemma of using either arbitrary allocations or unmeasurable bases for allocation are: 1) avoid allocations by measuring residual asset valuations in terms of market prices at the end of

each period; 2) attempt no allocations and present cash flow and funds statement instead of income statements; or 3) select uniform methods of allocation on the basis of their ability to permit predictions, regardless of inherent logic. Research has as yet been unable to provide acceptable support for any one of these alternatives.
          —Eldon S. Hendricksen, *Accounting Theory*

Upon the completion of a multiple-choice quiz concerning the above paragraph, I solicit individual reactions to this reading assignment. While the responses take various forms, the vast majority of them are overwhelmingly negative:
"I *do* like to read, but I didn't like reading *that*."
"I don't know anything about business; therefore, I couldn't relate to it."
"I just didn't feel like reading right now."
"That was something I, personally, would not have selected."
"That passage was *boring*!"
Through this rather unpleasant little task, a flash of insight usually occurs. So *this* is what we do to children when we "force" a basal reader story upon them! How can *we* know when children feel like reading?! From these new understandings comes a new, more puzzling question: Why, then, do we continue clinging so tenaciously to the basal reader when we have good reason to believe it does not provide for the diverse backgrounds and current interests of each of our students?
I have asked this very question informally of dozens of classroom teachers in the past ten years, and have received the following unvarying responses, which perhaps we can consider as "reasons *for* using a basal reader":

1.   A basal reader provides a systematic, sequential development of all the necessary reading skills;
2.   The basal is usually accompanied by a structured, easy to use teacher's guide, which provides lesson plans, questions to ask, and many helpful suggestions;
3.   The introduction of new vocabulary words is carefully controlled and reinforced in basal readers;
4.   Most basal readers offer a wide variety of high quality literature selected by experts in the field of education.

On the other hand, some teachers interviewed mentioned certain drawbacks that they had found in the use of basal readers, in addition to those that have already been mentioned:

1. Traditional use of the basal reader tends to hold some children back, doomed to the laborious practice of skills they have long ago mastered; while slower children may be pushed ahead of what for them would be a "comfortable pace."

2. Basals, used for traditional skill grouping, don't always provide for the differences in interest that begin to emerge between boys and girls at the ages of about nine or ten.

3. Because they revere the "authority" of the instructional guide accompanying the basal, many teachers feel reluctant to deviate from the guide, when their particular class tells them other activities might be more appropriate.

An answer to the limitation of the basal reader is appearing in the '90s, as educators have begun to realize that the *content* of what is read is at least as important as the *process* used in teaching reading. More and more, children's literature is finally finding its way into the elementary classroom to supplement the basal reader. For example, in California, teachers are required to teach units based upon quality literature that is suggested by the State Department's *Recommended Readings in Literature: Kindergarten Through Grade Eight* (California State Department of Education, 1986). Other states are following California's lead and recommending that children's literature be used in the classroom (Norton, 1992). In fact, interest in "authentic" reading material seems to be mushrooming. Writers of an article in *Reading Today* mused that ". . . everywhere you look, there seems to be a renewed interest in the use of children's literature in the school reading program. This trend is evidenced by increased coverage of the topic in conference presentations, journal articles, and books" (Miller & Luskay, 1988).

This book was created to propose an alternative, literature-based approach to teaching reading, while still maintaining those positive characteristics of a basal reader that are considered most important to its proponents. The following chapters will explore a host of suggestions and innovative ideas that have as their ultimate goal increased motivation to read for pleasure, yet the "hit or miss" quality of many "free" reading programs has scrupulously been avoided.

Realistically, the teacher must be held accountable for the students' skill development. With this fact in mind, the following pages will explore a program designed to provide students with the compendium of skills necessary to decode independently and think critically. This program was mostly created, however, to help children to view reading as a very pleasant activity to be pursued diligently, far beyond the classroom doors.

The target of these chapters is those teachers and educators who feel constrained by the basal reader, and/or for those creative (and brave) souls who feel open to new ideas and activities that might work better for their particular class than the "assembly-line," generic ideas offered by basal authors. Finally, the book is intended for those individuals who genuinely love reading themselves and believe that the task of creating readers who willingly *do* read is at least as important as producing ones who *can* read, but don't. Although what is proposed on the following pages is an alternative approach to the basal reader, the yet unconvinced reader who would prefer to keep the "security" of the basal, but who is interested in adding zest to the total reading program, is eagerly solicited. You, too, may find the suggestions equally helpful and challenging, and ... who knows? You may soon voluntarily relinquish your "tried and true" basal reader!

References

Anderson, R.C., et al. (1985). *Becoming a Nation of Readers: The Report of the Commission on Reading*. Champaign, IL: The Center for the Study of Reading.

Busch, F. (1972). "Basals Are Not For Reading." In *The First R: Readings on Teaching Reading*, edited by S. L. Sebesta and C. J. Wallen. Chicago: Science Research Associates.

California State Department of Education. (1986). *Recommended Readings in Literature: Kindergarten Through Grade Eight*. Sacramento, CA: State Department of Education.

Hendricksen, E.S. (1970). *Accounting Theory*. Homewood, IL: Richard D. Irwin.

Johnson, C. (1963). *Old Time Schools and School Books*. Dover Publications.

Meisel, S., and G.G. Glass. (1970). "Voluntary Reading Interests and the Interest Content of Basal Readers." *The Reading Teacher* 28, March, pp. 655-659.

Miller, M., and J. Luskay. (1988). "School Libraries and Reading Programs Establish Closer Ties." *Reading Today.* 5, 1, p. 18.

Norton, D.E. (1992). *The Impact of Literature-Based Reading.* New York: Merrill.

Pieronek, F.T. (1980). "Do Basal Readers Reflect the Interests of Intermediate Students?" *The Reading Teacher* 31, January, pp. 408-411.

Smith, L.B. (1980). "The Ideal Reading Program: One Teacher's Vision." *Instructor*, May, pp. 37-39.

Chapter One

Setting Up An Affective Reading Program

I have learned . . . that the head does not hear anything
until the heart has listened . . .
—James Stephens, *The Crock of Gold*

Recently, I came upon a phrase in James Stephens' book *The Crock of Gold* that reflects "I have learned . . . that the head does not hear anything until the heart has listened . . ." The sentiment instantly struck a resounding chord: what is really being advocated on these pages is a reading program directed toward the "heart," or in educational jargon, the affective domain, rather than solely for the "head," or the cognitive domain. With this new flash of inspiration, the name of the new program became Affective Reading to call attention to its predominant emphasis on creating readers who will one day leave school with a lifelong love of books. They will hopefully be readers who love reading because it is an activity that has often made them feel good. The term may also serve to distinguish the program from its predecessor, "Individualized Reading" which, continuing with Stephens' metaphor, was too often concerned with teaching the "head" to read when maybe the "heart" wasn't really listening.

An Affective Reading Program is really a combination of several approaches, some new and some "tried-and-true," that come together to form a dynamic way for children to learn to read as pleasurably as they have recently learned to talk. The program has the following features and beliefs:

1. Motivation is the linchpin to success in any reading program;
2. Children will be much more motivated to read what they have selected themselves;
3. Skills of reading should be taught as needed, but not indiscriminately;
4. There are appropriate times in a reading program for individual reading, group sharing, and whole class activities;
5. The teacher and child as partners should discuss the strengths and weaknesses of each individual reading "performance";
6. "Practice makes perfect" in reading as in other activities that children naturally enjoy;

7. Teachers must genuinely love reading and believe in its value in order to effectively model "reading behavior";
8. Teachers *can* teach effectively without a basal reading series.

For maximum success in an Affective Reading Program, a large block of time is required. However, many of the components of the language arts are so indelibly intertwined with the program that they could also be considered part of the language arts, and therefore afforded time accordingly, if a structured curriculum demanded it. Affective Reading is a truly "whole language approach" to reading.

An Affective Reading Program might ideally consist of the following components: 1) A one-hour block of time in which children are mainly reading silently the books they have chosen, writing or planning follow-up activities to reading, or meeting individually to read aloud to the teacher; they may also choose to read with partners, or meet in small discussion groups to share their ideas about what has been read with children who have chosen the same book; 2) A half-hour segment is set aside for small skill group instruction as needed, for the sharing of follow-up activities, and for special reading interest groups. On other days in this same time frame, the class might meet as a whole to write poetry or dramatic scripts, or to share follow-up activities geared for larger audiences. Additionally, two more fifteen or twenty-minute time allotments are set aside daily for 3) instructional cloze lessons and 4) for the teacher to read aloud to the children (see diagram A).

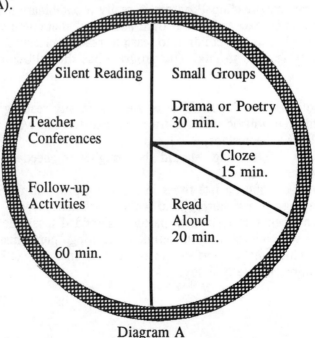

Diagram A

Obtaining Books

Though Affective Reading does not need extensive funds in order to get it going, it does require books—lots of them!—to accommodate the crucial free-reading portion. Some teachers may also wish to utilize other reading material, such as comic books, manuals, magazines, cereal boxes, etc., but my personal feeling is that today, with so very many enticing children's books in print, a sufficiently large selection of trade books can be offered to appeal to every child's interest, and give children the real experience of reading the foremost reading vehicle—THE BOOK. Tradebooks also have these distinct advantages:

1. They are the finished product of creative artists;
2. They (usually) deal with only one concept or idea;
3. They are often charming, as they must sink or swim on their own charm;
4. No one HAS to read them;
5. Each one is meant for a "special" reader.

(Veatch, 1967)

A full classroom library of trade books can be acquired in many inexpensive ways. Since Affective Reading insists that the children are involved in planning and selecting their own programs, they might be first asked to bring in their favorite books, or ones they have already read, from home. A book swap generates enthusiasm and can be conducted every month or so. Commercial book clubs offer paperback books at reasonable prices for students and also provide free bonus books for the classroom library. Parent groups can often be encouraged to raise funds for the purpose of supplementing classroom libraries, and never forget garage and yard sales as *the* source of bargains in used books. Frequent outings to the public library can begin a good habit and also yield five or six books per student to be circulated around the room. The cooperation of the school librarian, of course, will be crucial to the program. Most librarians will allow the teachers to take out many books for classroom circulation in addition to those the children borrow. Moreover, some librarians can be persuaded to visit classrooms every so often to give brief chats about their favorite books from the school library. These "book buildups" usually arouse the interest of many listeners, especially if back-up copies are brought along to be signed out on the spot. Book Fairs, coordinated by the librarian and/or reading teacher(s), can create a heightened enthusiasm for buying and reading books, often to the point of starting a reading epidemic in the school.

Lastly, it is actually possible to get matching funds for a free book distribution program for students through "Reading Is *Fun*damental." This federally funded program, which involves only a minimum of red tape and little additional work on the part of the teachers, demands only that three book distributions are instituted each year and that each child is given at least three free books in a year. The beauty of this program is that, unlike Book Fairs, it does not discriminate against poorer children and, unlike borrowing library books, the children actually *own* the books and can be encouraged to start personal libraries. More information about this unique program can be obtained from:

> The Field Staff
> Reading is *Fun*damental, Inc.
> Smithsonian Institute
> L'Enfant 2500
> Washington, D.C. 20560

Matching Books to Readers

One year, while teaching reading in a junior high school, I was amazed at the number of students who admitted that they had never voluntarily read a whole book before, but who eagerly devoured many books when the right child and the right book were brought together, along with an allotted time just to read. As this scenario is fairly typical, "matching books to readers" is a pivotal part of the Affective Reading Program. Although the program insists that children be allowed to choose what they wish to read, initially children may need guidance in the following two areas:

Rule of Thumb. Children must learn to select books which are not too difficult for them. Although there is some truth to the notion that a child can read a book above his or her reading level if interest in the topic is sufficiently heightened, this situation runs the risk of frustrating the child. Frustrated often enough, a child will "turn off" reading forever. Therefore, to practice reading comfortably and efficiently, the book chosen must *never* be too difficult. Children must be taught and urged to practice the "Rule of Thumb" which asks them to: Choose a page in the middle of a book they would like to read. Read the whole page as they use the fingers of one hand to count the number of words unfamiliar either in meaning or pronunciation. If more than five such words are encountered, the book is probably too difficult to be read comfortably and an easier one should be selected.

On the other hand, there is no such thing as a book that is too easy and this should be strongly put across to the students. Indeed, a book below a child's reading level provides useful practice in fluency, rate, and increases confidence and enjoyment in reading. Thus, aside from discouraging children from trying to read books which are too hard, they should be allowed to pace themselves. Leave the "challenges" to Pac Man!

Gauging Interests. It may seem strange, but it cannot be assumed that children will automatically know how to choose books that will be of interest to them. They are often enticed by pictures, the color of the cover, the size of the print, the number of pages, or many other extraneous factors that may lead them to select a book that, once chosen, has no deeper appeal to them. Therefore, at the start of the program it is important to obtain some information on the specific reading interests of every student in the class in order to lead them to books they may like.

More studies have been conducted on the topic of children's reading interests than on almost any other subject in reading. The resultant information can be of some help in purchasing trade books for the classroom, but the best way to find out what each child in *your* class is interested in reading about is to ask each one individually. This can be done utilizing a Reading Interest Inventory. The following is an example of such an inventory that might be used to focus in on possible reading interests of a child.

At first, children might be guided to several books on some topics that would seem appropriate according to their expressed interest on the inventory, and they could be encouraged to choose one of them. The teacher can then assist the child in applying the rule of thumb to the book selected.

Additionally, whenever books are completed, children should be encouraged to "rate" the book on a paper attached to the back cover using a simplified scale: super *****; very good ****; good ***; fair **; terrible *. Soliciting children's ratings shows respect for their opinions and also gives other possible readers some idea of the reaction of their peers.

Interest Inventory

_____   _____
Name of Child   Birthdate

_____
Grade

Do you like school? Why or why not? _____

What do you like best about school? _____

What do you like least about school? _____

What do you like to do in your free time? _____

What TV programs do you like to watch? _____

What games or sports do you like? _____

Do you have any hobbies? _____

Do you take any special lessons? _____

What would you buy if you had a million dollars? _____

Do you have any pets? If not, would you like one? _____

What do you and your friends like to do? _____

What do you want to be when you grow up? _____

Do you have any books at home? _____

What do you like to read about? _____

What is the best book you ever read? _____

Do you go to the library? _____

Do you read outside of school? When? _____

How do you feel about reading? _____

Do (did) your parents ever read to you? _____

Do (did) you like being read to? _____

Is reading easy or hard for you? Why? _____

Selecting Books

The actual process of selecting books both from the classroom and from the library can be a time of exciting intellectual interchange, where the teacher gives assistance and advice as needed, but is mostly on the scene to praise selections and to make appropriate comments that show respect for the child's opinion about "what is good to read." Instead of tedious library lectures on the Dewey Decimal System or the intrigues of the card catalogue, children should come to view the library with affection, as the "house of books." They can then be taught specific library skills as they begin to ask questions about where to find specific books or topics. When they are more focused and no longer content to merely browse and select hit-or-miss fashion, they will be much more receptive to learning the particulars of using the library.

Thus, with plenty of books in the classroom library as well as time allotments just for reading, certain decisions must now be made by the teacher. The following seven areas might be considered before implementing an Affective Reading Program. The first three will be dealt with in the remainder of this chapter, while the last four will be discussed in chapter three.

1. *Personalized reading follow-up activities.* What kinds of purposeful language arts activities should be offered to children to extend the experience of the book just read and to encourage others to read it?

2. *Small group activities.* When and how should small groups be formed for specific skill instruction, sharing of books, or broadening reading interests?

3. *Whole group activities.* For what purpose should the class come together as a whole for reading?

4. *Reading skills.* What are the important reading skills needed for powerful reading, and how and where will they be acquired?

5. *Student/teacher conferences.* What accommodations should be made for the diagnostic listening to each child's oral reading?

6. *Record keeping.* What kind of records should be kept by the teacher and students to keep track of reading progress?

7. *Evaluation.* How can the teacher be sure each student has read and adequately comprehended the books? Must the teacher have read all the books used in the program?

Personalized Activities

To enrich the experience of a book just read, as well as to provide a vehicle through which to invite others to read it, children will enjoy engaging in a variety of self-selected post-reading activities designed to complement *any* book read. Besides these benefits, such activities create an atmosphere of enthusiasm and also give students an option for those times when they just "don't feel like reading." A child may choose to read several books in succession while on a "reading roll" or, similarly, opt to do several activities before again settling down to the more sedentary pleasure of reading. As all the post-reading activities recommended here involve a good bit of high level thinking, writing or oral language skills, they are reinforcing reading skills indirectly and, as such, also reinforce the total reading program. If, however, a child seems to be deliberately avoiding reading for an extended period of time, the teacher might informally talk to him or her and attempt to get to the root of the problem, and perhaps gently guide the child toward a choice of tempting books on his or her interest and reading level.

The following ideas are only a few possible activities that teachers and students have devised for use in various programs:

1. *Predictions*. A child reads all but the last chapter of a book, writes a new version of what might happen in the last chapter, and then finishes the book to compare the two endings.

2. *Update*. For books that are historical in nature, the child writes a new "ultra-modern" version, perhaps using "Valley Girl" lingo, for example.

3. *Similar story*. Using the same characters, the student writes a story of their further adventures (this is especially good for a book that the child hated to see end).

4. *Different setting*. The child rewrites the story line; this time it takes place on the moon, in the desert, in the jungle, etc.

5. *Autobiography*. The story is retold for a small group of children from the point of view of one of the minor characters.

6. *Who should read this?* The child selects a famous person—historical or contemporary—whom he or she feels ought to have read the book and explains why.

7. *Rewrite the book*. The child prepares to read the story for a much younger audience, rewrites it accordingly, and then actually reads it to younger students. Great self-concept booster!

8. *Who said it?* Colorful quotes from the characters in the book are copied onto note cards. The characters are vividly described to the class and then they must guess who said it.

9. *Skit*. A script is written about a funny or exciting part of the book. The skit is then cast by the reader using classmates. The reader "stars" or "directs."

10. *Chalk-talk*. The child tells other students about the whole book, or an especially exciting chapter, using colored chalk on the blackboard to make accompanying sketches.

11. *Mural*. Scenes from the book are painted on roll paper by several students who have read the book. Captions are created for each scene.

12. *Letter to the author*. A letter is written to the author (in care of the publisher) describing what children liked about the book, suggestions for other books they would like to see the author write, or something that bothered them about the book. A reply causes a surge of interest in other books by the author.

13. *Exam*. A student creates ten thought-provoking questions about the book. Others who read it may answer them "for fun" and the "examiner" gets to correct them.

14. *Advertisement*. The student makes an advertising campaign for the book, exaggerating its glamorous parts as movie ads might. Great for critical thinking skills.

15. *Invitation*. A formal invitation (to be displayed in a prominent place in the room) is written, enticing others to read the book. Calligraphy and/or gold or silver ink may be used to enhance motivation.

Small Group Activities

As an important adjunct to the Affective Reading Program, adequate time should be set aside for small group activities. These groups might be formed for the purpose of introducing or reinforcing skills to a group of students, which will be discussed in detail in chapter three, as well as for sharing some of the personalized post-reading activities, and for special reading interest groups. What is to be stringently avoided is the rigid ability group that not only stigmatizes lower-ability children but has historically tended to "track" culturally and linguistically diverse learners.

Sharing Groups. Some of the post-reading activities just described ideally require an audience to create maximum enthusiasm. Sharing groups may thus be formed on a voluntary basis. A "Chalk Talk" that has been authored by a student just finishing *Charlotte's Web*, for example, might be an enjoyable activity for that student to perform for the benefit of six or seven youngsters who are wondering if this might be a good book for *them* to read.

Interest Groups. My own experience tells me that people's interest in reading is often as unique and individual as they are. I therefore question whether anyone should be coerced to cease reading only sports stories, for example, if this is the genre that gives him or her the most pleasure. On the other hand, children sometimes avoid reading certain types of books, only because they have never had any experience with the new topic and simply feel more comfortable with the "known." Jigsaw Grouping (Spiegel, 1981) might be useful for introducing children to other areas that could be of interest.

In Jigsaw Grouping, the entire class is temporarily divided into five or six groups, according to the current interests of its members. One class might decide, for example, to have a dinosaur group, a baseball group, an Indian group, a horse group, and perhaps a stamp collecting group. In phase one of Jigsaw Grouping, members of each of these groups would discuss and pool their knowledge on the chosen subject, and later decide on a list of questions they would like to have answered.

Questions would then be divided up and each member would use the library (and the librarian or other resource persons) to find their answers. Back in their groups and armed with some new insights, each group writes a report together, adding illustrations where appropriate.

The second phase of jigsaw grouping requires that new groups be formed which would now include one member of each of the former interest groups. In other words, each new group would consist of one person from the dinosaur group, one from the baseball group, one from the Indian group and so forth. The group reports on each topic are shared with the new group, thus allowing each group member to learn a bit about four possibly unfamiliar topics as well as having a time in the spotlight as an expert. In this way, interest can be aroused to read about something new and self-concept for *all* readers is increased.

Strategy Groups. Children for whom English is a second language may be put in a group in which there will be much discussion on a topic so that standard English will be modeled effusively; similarly, some children for whom the strategy of thinking critically is not fully utilized will benefit from being in a group of readers who can model this strategy by thinking aloud (Flood, Lapp, Flood, & Nagel, 1992).

Random Groups. Sometimes, to avoid stigma and to give children exposure to other children with whom they have never been grouped, numbering children off and putting all the same numbers together in groups provides a refreshing way for children to come together for literacy instruction (Flood, Lapp, Flood, & Nagel, 1992).

Whole Group Activities

To foster class cohesiveness and to provide group activities from which all students can benefit, there will be many times when the class can work together as a whole on activities that develop reading ability. To ensure that students across all reading levels have access to the book that is chosen, an affective teacher will want to use an approach that provides a "scaffold", or temporary structure, to support children's success in a text that may be too difficult (Bruner, 1978). For example, the teacher might use the following creative techniques suggested by Tompkins (1992):

1. Tell the story of the book in your own words or dramatize it before children read it. Because this technique is so motivational, children will be more excited about reading the book, and the drama or recitation will give them a set of expectations about the text.

2. Use an easier book on the same topic. Particularly with nonfiction material, tradebooks can be found with a variety of reading levels. Allow less capable readers to read a book with the same theme while the teacher reads the chosen book aloud.

3. Have the children read the book more than once. With repeated readings children glean more and more of the messages and subtle meanings in a text. Limited English speakers pick up more and more new vocabulary.

4. Tape-record the book. Children especially appreciate a story that has been recorded in the teacher's own familiar voice, or a child who needs practice in fluency may record the book. As children listen and follow along with their own copy of the book, their confidence and competence increases—more so with a second and third reading.

5. Pair less capable readers with more capable readers. Children can be paired across grade levels or in the classroom using this highly motivational approach. As an extension, the pair can write their responses to the book in "buddy journals" (Bromley, 1989), in which they write back and forth to each other any of their reactions to the book.

Another such activity might be for a highly motivational lesson using the cloze procedure, which will be explained in chapter eight. Other events which may include the entire class could be the writing and sharing of poetry (chapter five), as well as writing and performing dramatic scripts (chapter six). Additionally, certain post-reading activities, might be deemed by students and the teacher to be worthy of the attention of the total class.

Finally, every Affective Reading Program *must* include a daily read-aloud component. Fifteen or twenty minutes set aside for the teacher to read to the whole class can help to widen the interests of the students as well as provide an opportunity for students to demonstrate their love of reading by sharing a book they particularly enjoy. Too often teachers cease reading to children after the primary grades, assuming that as soon as children can read independently, they don't need this activity anymore. Nothing could be further from the truth! Besides the obvious motivational factors of a read aloud activity, done consistently, it also helps to develop reading skills. To illustrate, research conducted by Carbo (1978) revealed that an experimental group of twenty classes of seven-year-olds read to on a daily basis were significantly ahead of the control group, who were not read to, on measures of reading vocabulary and comprehension.

Summary

What has been proposed in the preceding pages is an Affective Reading Program designed to allow children to view reading as an enjoyable activity. It offers built-in provisions for ample reading practice, so that children can actually apply the skills of reading in a way that appeals to their hearts—by reading books that are personally meaningful to them because they alone have chosen to read them.

Enrichment activities, also self-selected, have also been included to help the children to go beyond the printed page with their thinking, as well as to allow them to share their most pleasurable reading experiences with others. Finally, a variety of small group, whole group, as well as personalized reading and writing activities are suggested to allow for variety in the program and to provide the kinds of stimulating activities that create an exciting atmosphere in the classroom. The program is relatively easy to supervise, obviously fun for children, and reaches them right where they are in reading and then helps them to develop as active and powerful readers. Just how the underlying reading skills are acquired "painlessly" will be dealt with in the next two chapters.

References

Bromley, K.D. (1989). "Buddy Journals Make the Reading-Writing Connection," *The Reading Teacher* 43, 122-129.

Bruner, J.S. (1978). "The Role of Dialogue in Language Acquisition." In A. Sinclair, R.J. Jarvella, and W.M. Levelt (eds.) *The Child's Conception of Language,* pp. 241-256. New York: Springer-Verlag.

Carbo, M. (1978). "Teaching Reading with Talking Books," *The Reading Teacher* 32, no. 3, December, 267-273.

Flood, J., D. Lapp, S. Flood, and G. Nagel. (1992). "Am I Allowed to Group Using Flexible Grouping Patterns for Effective Instruction?" *The Reading Teacher* 45, 8, 608-616.

Spiegel, D.L. (1981). *Reading for Pleasure: Guidelines.* Newark: International Reading Association.

Stephens, J. (1940). *The Crock of Gold.* New York: The Macmillan Company.

Tompkins, G.E. (1992). "The Scaffolding Principle: What to Do When the Book Is Too Difficult," *The California Reader*, vol. 25, 170. 3, 7-12

Veatch, J. (1968). *How to Teach with Children's Books.* New York: Citation Press.

White, E.B. (1952). *Charlotte's Web.* New York: Harper & Row.

Chapter Two

Creating a Positive Classroom Climate

The deepest principle of human nature is the craving to
be appreciated.

—William James

A medical doctor quickly picks up on the general well-being or
malaise of a patient, even before he has made a thorough diagnosis. In
a similar vein, it is usually possible to get a very quick, yet strong
reading as to how children feel about themselves as learners within a
classroom if one is a sensitive observer.

As a professor of education, one of my favorite duties is the
supervision of student teachers, which gives me ample opportunity to
observe children in a variety of classroom settings. On a typical day, I
walk into Miss Craig's room and I am barely noticed, so engrossed are
the students in writing a group story about Leonard's new baby sister.
The children are eagerly involved, yet noticeably relaxed, and everyone
giggles (including the student teacher) when Leonard remarks that the
infant is as "bald as a baseball." I find myself laughing with them, and
wish I didn't have to leave. Next door, however, Mrs. Kendall is
conducting her more traditional reading groups. The children in one
group are squirming uncomfortably as Ryan stumbles through a passage
about the coastline of Argentina. Josh, in the independent workbook
group, is entertaining Kate and Sarah by depressing his nose each time
the horn beeps on a truck out in the street. The teacher is not amused,
and hastily puts the names of Josh, Kate, and Sarah on the board. The
three "culprits" begin to sulk. Ryan, meanwhile, bites his lip and stares
at me suspiciously, as if I am somehow to blame.

Though one is always aware of the "aura" of classrooms on a
subliminal level, it is sometimes difficult to put into words the
"something" that makes the students in one classroom so animated, so
accepting of themselves and others and eager to learn. On the other

hand, it becomes clear so quickly in a neighboring room that the students would prefer to be somewhere—anywhere—else.

As a positive classroom climate is so fundamental to the development of an Affective Reading Program, I have for several years taken note of what I have determined to be the most necessary environmental factors for such a program. While it is by no means an exhaustive list, I have identified the major traits of the happiest, most inviting classrooms I have observed:

- Children have a choice of activities and materials.
- Many provocative questions originate from the children.
- Plenty of praise and appreciation is shown.
- Children get help from other children during seat work.
- A "soft buzz," as opposed to "total silence," is heard.
- Teachers and students frequently laugh together.
- Risk taking (i.e. taking a "stab" at difficult questions) occurs.
- There is eye contact between participants as they speak.
- Children are "on task," or working purposefully, most of the time.
- Interesting things to read and examine are displayed around the room.
- Children's "best work" is on display in a prominent place.
- "In jokes" are shared between teacher and pupils.
- A spirit of cooperation, rather than competition, is in evidence.

The Nature of an Affective Reading Program

Besides the above attributes, an affective reading program is one in which reading, writing, listening and speaking are kept "whole" rather than in fragmented skill units. These activities are done for real purposes rather than for artificial "workbook" reasons. For example, children read for enjoyment and to learn rather than to answer multiple-choice questions; they write letters, stories, and poetry to communicate rather than to practice subskills in rote fashion. And finally, in an affective reading program the quality and quantity of "talk" is very different from that found in traditional classrooms. Children are encouraged to talk about what they are doing, to discuss misunderstandings, and to solve problems in pairs or small groups. Constant discussions about books in an affective reading program stimulates interest, involvement and clarifies ideas. Just as children talk about their reading, they also discuss their writing to try out their ideas and get feedback about their works-in-progress. This continuous "talk" not only provides the most ideal atmosphere for a non-native speaker to acquire English, but it also expands a child's theory of the world, and increases his/her ability to remember (Staab, 1991).

Since it is often difficult to evaluate an atmosphere in which one is so closely intertwined, it may be helpful to have a respected colleague observe the classroom to decide whether or not the above things are happening and the climate is especially inviting to children. Sometimes an outsider can more objectively use the preceding guidelines to help answer the question: Are my students in a classroom where they are helped to become happy and eager to learn?

Student Assessment

A more direct way to assess the classroom climate is to ask children themselves specific questions regarding their perceptions of the classroom, the teacher, and their classmates. This technique not only shows respect for the ideas and opinions of the children, but it may also allow the teacher to gain new insights into the attitudes of those individuals most reticent about revealing their feelings about the classroom.

The following tool, or one adapted to reflect each classroom's special characteristics, can help the teacher to get a quick overview of the general classroom climate. If the students can already read, they may need only brief instructions to answer "quickly and honestly"; for nonreaders or beginning readers, the teacher might read the items orally and then let the students select their answers by using happy or sad faces.

My Classroom

Please read these sentence beginnings and finish them in a way that best tells how YOU feel about your classroom.

1) When I think of coming to this classroom, I think of
   a. all good things
   b. mostly good things
   c. some good things and some bad things
   d. mostly bad things

2) When I'm in this class, I
   a. usually feel wide awake and very interested
   b. am pretty interested, but sometimes bored
   c. am not interested and bored lots of the time
   d. don't like it and am always bored

3) When I'm in this class, I feel like I want to try
   a. very hard
   b. quite hard
   c. not very hard
   d. not hard at all

4) I get to ask questions in this class
   a. a lot
   b. sometimes
   c. once in a while
   d. never

5) Most of the other students in this class feel
   a. happy to be here
   b. okay about being here
   c. not very happy to be here
   d. very unhappy about being here

6) If we help each other with our work at our seats, the teacher
   a. is very pleased
   b. doesn't mind it
   c. doesn't like it very much
   d. doesn't allow it at all

7) Learning from books in this class is
   a. fun
   b. okay
   c. not too good
   d. not fun at all

8) The way I read compared with the other students in my class is
   a. better than most
   b. about the same as most
   c. not as good as most
   d. much worse than most

9) When I'm in this class, I feel happy
   a. most of the time
   b. sometimes
   c. hardly ever
   d. never

10) The teacher and students in this class smile and laugh together
   a. most of the time
   b. sometimes
   c. hardly ever
   d. never

11) The students in this class act friendly toward one another
   a. always
   b. most of the time
   c. sometimes
   d. hardly ever

12) The teacher shows that (s)he understands how we feel
   a. always
   b. most of the time
   c. sometimes
   d. hardly ever

—adapted from Fox, Luszki, and Schmuck, 1966

The above informal diagnostic tool is not intended to be a precise instrument, but it may indicate areas needing attention. For example, if more than half of the class answered the last item "hardly ever," then the teacher may need to try to become more sensitive to the students' feelings by listening more and carefully considering their concerns. On the other hand, if the majority of the students in the class feel that they are able to "ask questions a lot" (item 4) then the teacher can feel more confident that (s)he is giving them ample opportunity to initiate learning themselves.

The remainder of this chapter addresses in greater detail four areas that provide fertile soil in which the Affective Reading Program can best thrive.

Establishing Affective Relationships with Children

Any effort to establish a classroom climate that strives for mutual respect and the development of positive self-concepts may fail unless the teacher is able to build an accepting, affective relationship with the students.

To emphasize that this is not always as easy as it sounds, I often ask my preservice teachers if they value creativity and the right of each person to openly express his or her individuality. They all vehemently insist that they do. Then I ask them to tell me how they would feel if they were to sit on a bus next to a young man with a turquoise-blue, mohawk haircut. They balk! While this may be an extreme example, "teaching to the heart" demands that a teacher refrain from making value judgments and truly accept each child. Furthermore, the teacher must actively appreciate that which is unique about each child. It is crucial to free oneself of preconceived notions of how one believes children should "feel" and "think" and "look" in order to enter into the most beneficial kind of relationship with each child.

Specifically, it is important to do these things:

1. *Be respectful of the unusual questions children ask.* In some classrooms, many provocative questions are often ignored or actively discouraged because the teacher has deemed them off the object, or even "off the wall"! Every sincere question should be considered by the teacher.

2. *Show children that their own ideas have merit.* In many classrooms that are very teacher-centered, the children begin to believe that only "authorities" can have good ideas. When children are actively listened to by the teacher and each other, they grow in confidence in their ability to think and generate new ideas.

3. *Appreciate self-initiated learning.* In an Affective Reading Program much learning takes place independently via books that are self-selected. Therefore, children need to feel free to share their newly discovered ideas and reactions with the teacher and other students, and experience much praise and celebration.

4. *Provide many opportunities for children to read, think, and learn without the constant "threat" of evaluation.* Often children are afraid to think creatively because they are so anxious about tests and grades that any original thoughts are precluded. Children should feel free to explore unfamiliar territory without worrying about making "honest errors."

5. *In general, value that which makes each child unique.* Because there are so many children in an average class, there are many times when the teacher must ask them to conform. This can be counter-balanced by giving positive recognition to each child's special qualities—whether it be the child's dialect, hairstyle, smile, or even the way the child signs his or her name.

Making Learning a Cooperative Effort

When I was in high school, there was one girl who was deemed the best baby sitter in the town, in constant demand by all the parents. I asked her what it was that made her so popular and she replied, "I never TELL the children what to do. Everything is a two-way street: *We* have to pick up the toys now. *We* need to think of a game to play, etc." I have often thought about this baby sitter's method since that time, and I find it has some direct correlation to the classroom. Though *all* decisions cannot be made democratically, there are some activities that can take place cooperatively, with input from both the teacher and the students. Certain events can give the classroom more of a "we" feeling, as compared with a place that belongs to the teacher, and where students are passive "guests."

Grouping. There might be times during the day when students voluntarily leave the groups that were formed primarily for skill instruction. They can be helped to regroup in order to be with their friends (social grouping), or to share common reading and writing interests (interest grouping). Another alternative, "jigsaw grouping," was explained in chapter one as a way to develop new reading interests. Drama or poetry groups are other viable grouping options. Flexible grouping systems have several advantages for the development of self-esteem in the classroom: 1) they allow children to belong to several different groups of various abilities and interests; 2) they alleviate the ego-deflating stigma of children who are always members of the "slow" group; 3) they give children a choice of membership based on their own interests and special characteristics.

Children should also be encouraged to think of names for their newly formed groups. These group decisions build a cooperative spirit and a sense of belonging. Additionally, group leaders may be rotated so that each child has a chance to accept responsibility and feel "extra special."

Self-Monitored Progress. When children are actively involved in their own progress and evaluation, they feel much more in control of their learning, and are therefore much more motivated to succeed.

Cooperative evaluation techniques for reading will be discussed in chapter three, and these are invaluable in helping children to see where their strengths and weaknesses in reading lie. In addition, children can be made graphically aware of the gains they are making in reading by the use of self-monitored progress charts. Even primary-age youngsters can grasp the concept of a simple bar graph to color in, and they enjoy checking off skills as they are mastered, or sight vocabulary as it is committed to memory. More elaborate progress charts are often used as bulletin boards in elementary classrooms, but this practice is often a frustration for less able students whose progress may be steady, but slower. A more effective practice is to have them chart and try to better their *own* progress, to be shared only with the teacher and parents. Thus, they "compete" only with themselves.

Progress of the whole class, on the other hand, can most effectively be recognized on an attractive "Best Work" bulletin board, which continually gives students plenty of opportunity to display their finest efforts. As compared with a progress bulletin board that rewards "speed of achievement," every child can have something to say in written form that can be exhibited. Moreover, such a display board gives incentive for all children to rework their creative efforts into neat, mechanically perfect enterprises that children are truly proud to display.

Affirming with Word, Deed, and Touch

In general, the positive self-esteem of a child depends on whether that child is affirmed or infirmed, praised or belittled, recognized or ignored, and respected or ridiculed (Erickson, 1984). A classroom atmosphere that is characterized by appreciation for the child actually fosters self-esteem, as well as the achievement of the child's academic potential. However, without this appreciation, children often lack a keen interest in learning and can develop negative feelings about themselves.

Praise: Verbal Vignettes. The most important element in showing appreciation is sincere praise; it is probably the single most crucial factor in an Affective Reading Program. When I ask college students to think back to their fondest memories of their elementary school years, their most positive and vivid remembrances invariably concern a teacher showing his or her appreciation in the form of praise:

"My sixth grade teacher asked if she could send a copy of my poem to her mother."

"Mr. Thiems said I had natural ability in science."

"My teacher said I was a 'compassionate listener' and she liked that."

"I was told by my teacher one year that I had made more progress than anyone else."

"Mrs. Hall said she wished she was as creative as I was!"

"My second-grade teacher said she liked to listen to me read because I had a 'twinkly' voice."

Praise: Deeds. With other recollections, it was not what was said but the actions of the teacher, which literally "spoke louder than words."

"My teacher cared enough to come in a half hour early every morning to help me with my reading."

"Every so often I got 'happy notes' to take home that mentioned some good thing I had said or done during the day."

"My teacher really made us feel appreciated. She celebrated every child's birthday with a card, a cupcake, and a candle to blow out."

"One year we had a V.I.P. board. The children took turns bringing in their baby pictures and writing their autobiography to put up."

"Mrs. Wiegand took us to her house for a picnic at the end of the year. Boy, did we feel privileged!"

Praise: Touch. In spite of the recent concern about child abuse, children continue to crave affection from caring adults. Other college students remembered teachers because they were openly affectionate toward students, and showed them with a touch, a hug, or a gentle pat that they were very special people:

"One day I was feeling very dizzy. My teacher carried me into the teacher's lounge, put me down on the couch, and planted a concerned kiss on my forehead."

"When my father died, my teacher just squeezed my hand for the longest time without saying anything. I *knew* she understood."

"I remember the first book I ever read. When I finished the last page, the teacher hugged me and told me what a great accomplishment I had made...I read everything in sight after that!"

"I was so terribly shy, I was afraid to talk to the class. But my teacher held my hand while I talked to them, nodding and smiling all the while. I was never scared in that class again."

Summary

In order for an Affective Reading Program to flourish and produce readers who *want* to read and feel free to read critically, the classroom climate must be happy and accepting of each child as a unique individual. The self-concept of each child must be nurtured through encouragement and mutual respect so that students feel confident enough to explore and ask the questions that children so naturally formulate.

Though it is not easy to get an exact "reading" on the atmosphere in one's own classroom, positive behaviors of students that suggest a healthy classroom climate can be observed by the teacher, by a colleague, or by students themselves. When problem areas are identified, constructive steps can be taken to improve affective relationships with the students, so that they feel free to grow and learn in their own special ways. In addition, the classroom can become a more cooperative setting by working with children to help them choose membership in a variety of groups, and by allowing them to monitor their own academic progress.

Finally, the classroom climate can become one in which it is clear that children are appreciated, if praise is allowed to "run rampant." Children in an Affective Reading Program can be shown verbally, or by a thoughtful deed, or by a loving gesture, that they are "somebody special." The fact is, that they *are*. The distinct human potential of each child is *always* there, waiting to be discovered by some caring teacher and then invited forth.

References

Combs, A.W. (1982). *A Personal Approach to Teaching: Beliefs That Make a Difference*. Boston: Allyn and Bacon.

Cranfield, J., and H. Wells. (1976). *100 Ways to Enhance Self-Concept in the Classroom: A Handbook for Teachers and Parents*. Englewood Cliffs, NJ: Prentice-Hall.

Erickson, K. (1984). *The Power of Praise*. St. Louis: Concordia Publishing House.

Fox, R., M.B. Luszki, and R. Schmuck.(1966). *Diagnosing Classroom Learning Environments*. Chicago: Science Research Laboratory Associates, Inc.

Good, T., and J. Brophy. (1978). *Looking in Classrooms* (2nd ed.). New York: Harper & Row.

Grant, B.J., and D.G. Hennings. (1971). *The Teacher Moves: An Analysis of Non-Verbal Activity*. New York: Teachers College Press.

Purkey, W.W., and J.M. Novak. (1984). *Inviting School Success: A Self-Concept Approach to Teaching and Learning*. Belmont: Wadsworth Publishing Company.

Staab, C. (1991). "Talk in Whole-Language Classrooms." In V. Froese (ed.) *Whole-Language: Practice and Theory*. Boston: Allyn and Bacon.

Chapter Three

Providing for Skill Development and Evaluation

Making sense of print is what reading is all about.
    —K. Goodman, *Becoming a Reader*
        in a Complex Society

As compared with less "enlightened" times, hardly any practicing teachers today would fail to agree that the students in their classes are all unique individuals and that, ideally, each needs a different type and amount of instruction. In contrast to the classroom full of homogeneous, middle class learners that teachers could expect only a decade ago, teachers now will greet a diverse, heterogeneous garden of children from differing backgrounds, cultures, and linguistic groups.

Individualized instruction seemed the perfect remedy for some past ills in education, such as the Round Robin method. It arose in response to this emergence of the realization that there is a need for differentiated instruction, but the program itself eventually died out. Some say it didn't work because of the overwhelming amount of record keeping involved, while others have offered the observation that too many of the "individual" children were bored in their "individual" carrels and thus, were not attending to their "individual" work. In addition, many teachers admitted that they felt insecure without the expert guidance of their basal manual.

My own experience with that innovative movement of the seventies suggests that the major problems were often deeper than those just mentioned. Firstly, the individualized programs were not created *with* the student but *by* the teacher, who was too often concerned only with the rapid acquisition of a series of skills by the child. Secondly, the teacher did not always have a clear idea in mind of exactly which skills any given student needed. So, frequently *all* skills were taught to *all* students, whether needed or not. Finally, the goals of individualized reading programs were often to produce readers who *could* read, but seldom were provisions made to assure that children *would* read. For

31

example, the proponents of such programs did acknowledge that each child is an individual and must proceed according to his or her own rate. Children, therefore, were given individual programs of reading skills, yet the fact that each child also has unique reading interests, preferences, and attitudes was largely ignored. Individualized programs, in short, lacked appropriate consideration of the "heart" of each child.

The Affective Reading Program, by contrast, is designed to create readers who choose to read, mainly because they are free to choose *what* they read. Time is also set aside for sharing reading experiences in small groups and with the whole class to provide variety, as well as to allow the children some freedom as to when each activity shall be pursued. With an understanding of which skills should be nurtured for each child (which will be discussed in the rest of this chapter), teachers can then guide reading development naturally by listening to each child read self-selected material and "teaching" only as needed. The bottom line is that children learn to read by experience in reading. Affective Reading assures that children get that experience, and are not wasting time with drills on isolated skills for which they have not demonstrated a need.

Developing Reading Skills Naturally

Yes, Virginia, the skills of reading *can* be managed effectively without a basal teaching manual! Chapter four will explain how the word recognition skills can be introduced via a Language Experience Approach for beginning readers. When children have then acquired a sight vocabulary and some rudimentary skills with which to unlock new words, they are then ready to read simple trade books. They are then able to read independently with a minimum of assistance from the ever-watchful teacher.

First of all, it may be helpful for the teacher to put together a list of the most important word recognition skills as a frame of reference to determine what skills the child already has and which ones have yet to be acquired. I have included a compendium of such skills, which might prove useful for this purpose. Bear in mind, however, that none of these skills alone has been found to be a necessary prerequisite for reading success!

Word Recognition Skills Reference Sheet

I. Phonic Elements

_____   1. Identifies beginning consonant sounds in words
_____   2. Identifies middle consonant sounds in words

_____ 3. Identifies final consonant sounds in words
_____ 4. Identifies consonant combinations in words (e.g. "tr," "ch," "sn")
_____ 5. Can substitute beginning consonant sounds to form new words
_____ 6. Can substitute final consonant sounds to form new words
_____ 7. Identifies vowel sounds in beginning of words
_____ 8. Identifies vowel sounds at end of words
_____ 9. Identifies vowel combinations in words (e.g. "ai," "ou," "ei")
_____ 10. Identifies vowel sounds followed by "r" (e.g. "car," "fur," "born")
_____ 11. Other

II. Structural Analysis Skills

_____ 1. Divides words into units
_____ 2. Recognizes compound words
_____ 3. Recognizes contractions
_____ 4. Recognizes base (root) words
_____ 5. Recognizes common prefixes
_____ 6. Accents appropriate syllables when decoding new words
_____ 7. Recognizes possessive form of nouns
_____ 8. Other

III. Contextual Analysis Skills

_____ 1. Uses picture cues to decipher unfamiliar words
_____ 2. Uses the context to decipher unfamiliar words
_____ 3. Other

This list, or one with which the teacher feels most comfortable, can then be duplicated. A copy can be placed in the teacher's record keeping folder for each child, and another kept in each child's personal file so that as the skills are encountered and acquired, both the teacher and the child can check them off. Through wide reading, which is the basis of the program, many of the skills delineated above will be developed inductively without ever having been directly "taught." Some reading skills, for certain children, may require several examples and a bit of isolated practice before they can apply them. Making note of a particular decoding problem with several students, a teacher may wish to then hold a small group session with the students needing that skill work.

Often teachers feel worried about creating such skill lessons for students without the benefit of "prescriptions" suggested by a basal manual. They sometimes lament, "But *I* can't devise a phonics lesson; I don't even know a diphthong from a digraph!" Unfortunately this lack of confidence often prevents otherwise dynamic teachers from spontaneously providing specific lessons as they are needed in their classes. I assure teachers that if they themselves can and do read, and have a modicum of patience and common sense, then they can successfully guide students into making appropriate deductions about phonics and structural analysis without knowing all the fancy terminology. It is helpful to employ the following steps:

1) Determine (by listening to the child read orally) what reading skill is temporarily holding the child back;
2) Produce for the child several examples of words that illustrate the subskill;
3) Help the child to make the necessary generalizations about all the words;
4) Let the child practice on the subskill—only as much as is necessary; and
5) Allow the student to go back to his or her "real book" to apply the subskill.

To illustrate, a typical subskill problem that students might encounter could be identifying the vowel sound in the first syllable of a word such as "puppet," where the twin consonant in the middle gives the "u" a short sound. The teacher may gather together a group of students all experiencing similar difficulty. The teacher then writes on the board such words as "supper" and "super" for all to see. After a child in the group has successfully identified both words, the teacher asks the children to notice the difference in the spelling of the two words, as well as how these differences affect the vowel sound. Next, words such as "better," "wider," "hotter," "cuter," and "mutter"—all examples of the subskill being presented—are written and children are invited to verbalize how they now know the pronunciation of these new words in light of the previous examples. After more practice as needed, the group is disbanded as soon as each member has demonstrated sufficient understanding of the skill.

Teachers still not confident that they can generate such lessons themselves may refer to Heilman's *Phonics in Proper Perspective* or Durkin's *Strategies for Identifying Words*. Both are handbooks providing a host of ready-made lessons on every aspect of word recognition and can be adapted as teachers see fit. Additionally, Barnell Loft's *Specific*

Skill Series offers student work book activities on all phases and levels of reading skills. One of the skill booklets, "Working with Sounds," spans pre-reading through junior high level phonic and structural analysis skills and provides ample individual practice in each of these areas.

Many other word recognition skills will require only a brief comment, to be then applied and reinforced in the subsequent reading situation. Three days of intensive drill on compound words as often suggested by basal readers, in contrast, often seems a gross waste of a student's time when that student could be happily "practicing reading." I am reminded of an analogy offered by an infinitely wise professor, who asks if, after a young boy has just swum the English Channel, would one then demand that he go back and learn to "kick and blow bubbles," as these are subskills to swimming that he never mastered?!

Secondly, vocabulary words new in meaning, as well as "stickler" words that students consistently have trouble decoding, can be printed on 3x5 cards by the student as soon as such words are identified by either the student or the teacher. These words can be kept with the student in a word bank file with separate sections for new words, words from past lessons still needing review, and those that seem firmly integrated into the child's sight vocabulary.

For beginning readers, the pace at which new vocabulary is introduced can be controlled most efficiently, in this author's experience, through the use of Language Experience Stories, which will be discussed in the next chapter. This method complements an Affective Reading Program, as it insures that the first words that the children learn to read are those that they themselves have chosen. Thus, the words have the most meaning to them and are the easiest for them to remember.

Finally, while they are reading books they enjoy, children will at the same time be doing their own personal experiments with all aspects of decoding and encoding language. The trade book experiences provide abundant exposure to auditory perception via short stories where children must supply the rhyming couplets. Oversized print and repetition, so frequently found in children's literature, naturally aid in a child's acquiring and reinforcing basic sight vocabulary.

Shepherd (1975) contends that all the major areas of a complete reading and language program can be covered naturally through the use of trade books in the reading program. He specifically identifies six skill areas which are developed:

1. decoding and encoding skills
2. conceptual development
3. awareness of many patterns of grammar

4. awareness of the symbolic function of language
5. vocabulary expansion
6. flexibility of writing style and usage

Therefore, the role of the teacher who wishes to develop reading skills in an Affective Reading Program, is to allow children to discover reading on their own, but to be watching on the sidelines to step in and offer assistance when it is needed.

Student/Teacher Conferences

The brief conferences between teacher and student can be one of the most intimate and gratifying times of the day for both participants. The teacher is actually watching the child grow and learn, while most children delight in having the teacher's total attention centered on them for a few moments. Naturally, their effort is heightened. Usually lasting about three to five minutes a session, a conference should be scheduled once or twice a week for each child. Before each conference, students are instructed to select a passage or a page in the book they are reading that they especially liked or found amusing. With plenty of opportunity beforehand to "polish up the reading act," each child generally comes to the conference feeling confident and eager to "perform." The sessions may be taped as each child reads so that each child may later replay his or her tape. By following along while listening, children can then participate in their own evaluation, and also self-correct any errors noted. After children have finished reading, they are asked to tell briefly about what was read and then several probing questions are asked to determine their level of understanding.

Record Keeping

Some teachers thoroughly enjoy making charts and keeping highly elaborate records of anything and everything that happens in the classroom—from exactly how many repetitions a child made while reading orally to compiling a detailed list of just which books have been taken from the library, when, and by whom! But for those of you who find this tedious bookkeeping to be the very chore that keeps you clinging to your basal, take heart: An Affective Reading Program does not necessitate lengthy and laborious records; its success depends, rather, on brief qualitative remarks jotted down as the child reads to you. The following is an example of a Student/Teacher conference record for a typical second grade student:

CONFERENCE RECORD

Name: Elvira S.   Date: 9/23/86
Book: The Big Jump   Page(s): 30, 31

ORAL READING
   Much more fluent than 9/19. Beginning to read
more in phrases.
   Had some problems sounding out the "cr" in "crown"
but knew "gown." No more "then" and "when" confusion;
knew them both in context.

COMPREHENSION
   Rephrased the story perfectly for me! Got the main
idea which she has had trouble with before. Still just
uses mainly phonic cues, but is beginning to go back and
correct herself when words don't make sense in the
sentence.

COMMENTS & SUGGESTIONS FOR INSTRUCTION
   Very excited about this story—lead her to more fairy
tales in library!
   Making more attempts to guess unknown words
without me telling her.
   More and more expression in oral reading.
   Next time:
   1. Point out "cr" blend. Think of "cr" words
together.
   2. Review: gown, lake, crown.

The positive features are stressed and specific problems pointed out to the child at the end of the conference, and the teacher and student as partners work out a program to respond to deficiencies, if needed.

Evaluation

After a Student/Teacher Conference, the student plays back the recording of the passage that was just read, notes any difficulties, and reviews the new word cards made during the conference. In the cooperative climate fostered in an Affective Reading Program (chapter eleven), the children should feel free to ask other students words they have forgotten, if necessary, or put those words in the stickler file, to be discussed and reviewed at the next conference, or when the teacher is free.

Most teachers would agree that the ultimate goal of reading comprehension is of vital importance in any program. Therefore, the key competence for the teacher to develop is that of informal diagnosis. Besides noting and addressing any specific phonic errors, the teacher must learn to listen to a child's reading strategies to gain insight into how a child "thinks" when reading. It is helpful to determine if the child is just reading words and looking only for phonic cues to decode, or if a child is making "meaningful" errors based on understanding of grammar or—better still—based on the context of the other words in the sentence.

Example: I went to the ball game with my FATHER.

To illustrate, in the above sentence a child who reads the final word as "fat" is clearly paying attention only to the phonics, or the sounds and letters of the words. Such a child has not fully grasped the idea that grammatically, one would expect a noun—or more specifically a "person"—to end this sentence meaningfully. Another child reading the same word as "feather" is closer still in terms of phonic accuracy and has attended to the grammar needs of the sentence, but also is not concerned with the meaning of the sentence. A third child, who reads the final word as "Dad," is so thoroughly involved in the meaning of the sentence that he has "transcended phonics," and used his own familiar term for his "Dad." Though the last error is by far the least serious in terms of that child's total reading ability, unfortunately, it is the one most often "pounced upon" by well-meaning, but misinformed, teachers.

Comments as to which of these kinds of errors are consistently made are especially important and should be noted on each child's record sheet. Those which interfere with the meaning of what is read should be discussed with the child.

Informal Reading Inventories

To provide the teacher with further information about the child's reading, a device known as an informal reading inventory (IRI) may be used. This informal test consists of a series of graded passages which the child reads into a tape-recorder while the teacher codes his/her miscues using a kind of shorthand:

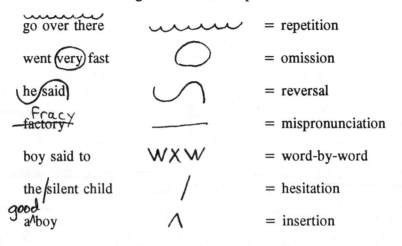

The inventory provides the teacher with information about the child's reading levels: independent, instructional, frustration, and listening capacity. The independent level is where very few errors are made, the child is reading fluently with excellent comprehension, and where the child could read the book by him/herself with no assistance. The instructional level is where the child may make some errors and would need instructional assistance from the teacher. The frustration level is to be avoided at all costs—if a child is continually asked to read material that is too difficult—judged by frequent word recognition errors, sketchy comprehension, sighing, and other nervous habits—that child may "turn off" to reading forever. Listening capacity, the fourth level, is the highest level at which the child could comprehend if he/she had all the necessary decoding skills.

To determine where to begin the IRI, children are asked to read a graded list of words. This pretest is terminated when the children reach a list in which they fail to correctly decode five words. The highest graded list of which the child said every word correctly determines the grade of the passage at which the teacher should ask the child to begin reading.

The child begins reading the beginning passage determined by the word list and then a series of comprehension questions are asked to the child. The child continues reading passages until his/her frustration level is reached. At that point, the teacher reads the following passage(s) to the child until that child reaches a point at which his/her comprehension falls to approximately 75 percent.

An affective teacher will then allow the child to go back and read the passage that precedes the first passage that (s)he read so that the child can leave the testing situation with a feeling of success rather than a sense of frustration.

The teacher then looks at his/her notes and determines where the child is comfortably reading: a child is said to be reading at the frustration level when recognition is below 90 percent and comprehension is 50 percent or below; to be at the instructional level, word recognition must be at least 95 percent and comprehension at least 90 percent; and for the book to be at the child's independent reading level, the word recognition should be 99 percent and the comprehension at or above 90 percent (Gunning, 1992). Obviously, such percentages are guidelines. Each child's frustration level is different and teachers should watch for such signs as frequent hesitations, stall tactics, hair twirling, sighing, and other affective measures to also determine how well the child is faring.

Informal reading inventories are available commercially. Among the most popular and easiest to administer is *Basic Reading Inventory* (Johns, 1991).

Questioning Techniques

Growth in comprehension also depends, to a large degree, on asking the "right" questions. It is not absolutely necessary for teachers to have read every single book that a child brings to a conference (though it doesn't hurt!). A quick look at the book, clues from the child, as well as astute listening to excerpts as several children read it are generally enough to enable a teacher to ask thought-provoking questions that will help to develop excellent comprehension skills. Past individualized programs often have not challenged a child to go beyond a literal recall of the book; comprehension skills of a more critical nature are an integral part of Affective Reading.

Analysis of a child's response to the question "What was the story about?" or "What was that author saying to you?" should provide a teacher with much important information about a child's sequencing skills, recall of details, ability to grasp the main idea, understanding motives of the characters, as well as the child's perceptions of the author's intent. This, however, is only the first step. Based upon the child's answers, open-ended questions can then be posed that inquire "How. . .?" "Why. . .?" "What if. . .?" or "What do you think. . .?" which lead to creative and critical levels of thinking, and also clearly place value on the child's own opinion. More prosaic questions that begin with "who, what, where, and when," on the other hand, can too often elicit shallow, one-word responses.

With books that the teacher has read, specific inference questions related to content or literary analysis can be written beforehand on cards and fastened to the book. The child may then come to the conference already prepared to answer them.

Literacy Profiles

Finally, to get an accurate picture of a child's development in both reading and writing, a helpful device for summarizing IRI information, conference notes, and the number of books read is the literacy profile (Gunning, 1992). This profile would not only include the above information, but also anecdotal information about the reader's prediction strategies, ability to use the context, skill at dramatizing a story, etc. The writing part of the profile would summarize the child's use of brainstorming strategies, understanding of story structure, facility with various model of discourse, and ease with the mechanics of language, for example. Because such a profile is not concerned with formalized test data, it puts a "human face" on the assessment task, and can be helpful in explaining progress to parents.

Summary

Hopefully, after reading this chapter you now feel somewhat more confident that you can provide your burgeoning readers with the underlying skill development that they need in a more natural, individualized fashion than with the "force-feeding" that is often advocated by basal readers. More will be said about the introduction of skills for beginning readers in the following chapter, and additional comprehension-building techniques will be provided in chapter five.

However, a final word of caution is offered here: the amount of word recognition skills needed by any one child is only the amount which allows that child to read independently—no more! Think for a moment about how you eventually got to be a decent tennis player (or skier or whatever). The initial motivation was there because you chose the activity, you learned a few moves, and then you practiced and practiced and PRACTICED. As you saw for yourself that you were becoming quite proficient, the practice became self-reinforcing. The final fluid performance came about by being able to do all the various little subskills without even thinking. Many of them you were never even taught. Now—if you had been constantly pestered to try to decide which hip moved up the slope when the pole was planted down the slope, and which ski to lift when, the anxiety produced by all that attention to mechanics might have ruined (or at least lessened) the beautiful feeling of the act as a *whole*. So it is with reading. Until your help is expressly needed, give your students the joyful experience of reading freely and unself-consciously for as long as they are able.

References

Boning, R.A. (1981). *Specific Skill Series*. New York: Barnell Loft, Ltd.

Durkin, D. (1982). *Strategies for Identifying Words*. Boston: Allyn and Bacon.

Goodman, K.S. (1984). "Unity in Reading." In A.C. Purves and O.S. Niles (eds.), *Becoming Readers in a Complex Society*. Third Yearbook of the National Society for the Study of Education, pp. 79-114. Chicago: University of Chicago Press.

Gunning, T.G. (1992). *Creating Reading Instruction for All Children*. Boston: Allyn and Bacon.

Heilman, A.W. (1985). *Phonics in Proper Perspective*. Columbus: Charles E. Merrill Publishing Company.

Johns, J.L. (1991). *Basic Reading Inventory* (5th ed.). Dubuque, IA: Kendall/Hunt.

Shepherd, D.L. (1975) "Individualizing Reading Instruction for High School Students," *High School Journal* 59, November, pp. 77-82.

Chapter Four

Emergent Literacy and the Language Experience

> . . . What a dangerous activity reading is: teaching is.
> All this plastering on of foreign stuff. Why plaster on at
> all when there's so much inside already? So much
> locked in? If only I could get it out and use it as
> working material. . .
>   —Sylvia Ashton Warner, *Spinster*

Perhaps the most important time of all to appeal to the hearts of children is when those children are first learning to read and forming their initial impressions of what reading is all about. Consider for a moment a child's first encounter with spoken language. From the child's own vast experience of listening to speech, a first word is chosen that has special meaning and warm associations for that child. Rarely are the words "come" or "look" or "see" chosen, as authors of basal readers seem to imagine, but rather "Mama," "Daddy," or someone or something close to that child's heart is usually the subject of the child's beginning verbal efforts.

Similarly, an Affective Reading Program might well be implemented with children learning to read and analyze words that they themselves have chosen via the language experience approach. As soon as the children have mastered enough words from reading their own stories, they can be gradually invited to read some self-selected beginner books—the more traditional format of written language.

The Language Experience Approach is based upon the following tenets:

1) Children learn best what is useful and meaningful to them;
2) Language experience is a multisensory approach and, as such, is a viable method for all kinds of learners;

3) Cooperation is stressed; competition is decreased; no one can "fail";
4) Children have a choice in what is read, and are not asked to learn just what the teacher decrees is of importance;
5) Both the teacher and the children can show appreciation at the end product (*everybody* took part in writing it);
6) Goals, progress, and evaluation are shared by the teacher and the children;
7) Feelings support thinking; Language Experience is an emotional approach that reaches the "whole" child.

(Lee and Allen, 1963)

The above tenets are obviously quite compatible with the goals and philosophy of Affective Reading and can provide a strong foundation from which to begin the other components of an affective program. Much research has been conducted on the effectiveness of the Language Experience Approach, mainly to see how it compares with basal reader instruction. While much of this research has yielded mixed results, programs that offer only this approach have usually been found to develop readers who achieve at least as well as those produced by basal readers, and in some cases, studies have shown that children taught by Language Experience were ahead of their basal reader counterparts in reading, writing, and attitude (Shapiro, 1991).

Specifically, the Language Experience Approach can be used with an entire class, or with smaller ability groups, and consists of these steps:

1. Provide a stimulus;
2. Have a group discussion about the stimulus;
3. Brainstorm with words and ideas;
4. Ask the children to make up sentences about the stimulus and write down what is said;
5. Read the story with the children;
6. Ask for volunteers to read individual sentences;
7. Ask for volunteers to identify specific words;
8. Give the story a title;
9. Make word cards and/or phonic element cards for specific skill work;
10. Duplicate the story and provide each child with a copy from which to start a "personal book."

The Stimulus

Often when students in my preservice reading classes are asked to demonstrate a simulated language experience story, they choose as their topics "A Trip to the Zoo," "The Three Ring Circus," "A Day at the Rodeo" or some other equally exotic topic. I tell them, "Keep in mind that children are utterly fascinated by the rainbow produced by the oily film on a mud puddle!" It is just these kinds of everyday mundane observations that can be a never-ending source of grist for the language experience mill. The stimulus can be *anything* that has recently been experienced by all members of the participating group. A Language Experience Story could be about a snowman made at recess, a seasonal thunderstorm, a television program that everyone happened to see, a new student, a story the class has just enjoyed listening to, or even about a fist fight that broke out on the playground. The single most important criterion is that the subject has captured the interest of the students and that they would like to talk about it, write about it, and read about it.

Discussion

Reading involves making associations between written words and spoken words. Therefore, a natural developmental bridge between the stimulus and reading about it is the oral discussion. After the group activity, the teacher will want to give the children an opportunity to share their reactions to the stimulus in their own words. The teacher's role is to listen, positively respond to discussants with appropriate comments (e.g. "So that snowman was much bigger than you thought he'd be, Johnny!"), and also to make sure all children get a chance to contribute if they wish.

Brainstorming

The brainstorming phase of the language experience is, unfortunately, the one most often neglected, but could be the step that ultimately gets children most interested in words as vehicles of self-expression and gets them organized to think creatively.

For example, after building a snowman together and a brief discussion of the experience, the teacher actively begins to guide the children into adding to their sight vocabulary by asking the students questions about the stimulus, like so:

1) Associations. "What kinds of things do we think of when we think about snowmen?" (winter, cold, fun, snow, etc.)
2) Description. "What words can we use to tell about snowmen?" (frosty, melting, freezing, funny, smiling, etc.)
3) Actions. "What kinds of things do snowmen do?" (melt, stand, smile, smoke a pipe, etc.)
4) Reactions. "How do snowmen make us feel?" (happy, cold, excited, proud, etc.)
5) Synonyms. "What other words can we use instead of 'snowman'?" (snow sculpture, snow statue, snow lady, etc.)
6) Antonyms. "What is something very different from a snowman?" (a scarecrow, a lifeguard, a snowflake, etc.) "Why?"
7) Comparison. "What is something else that is like building a snowman?" (building a snow fort, making a sand castle, etc.)
8) Beginning sounds. "What words can we think of that begin just like snowman?" (snow, snowing, snake, snail, etc.)

The responses to the brainstorming session are written by the teacher on the board and about eight to ten of the words, selected by the teacher, will later be written on cards by the children (or by the teacher at very early stages) as their new vocabulary words. Now the children are inspired to "write."

Dictation

When the activity has been discussed and many word possibilities are on the board for children to refer to, the teacher suggests that the class now write a story together about the stimulus and asks if anyone would like to contribute a "story beginning." Next, several more sentences are solicited to add to the story sequentially.

When the story has pretty much been recounted, the teacher asks the children for a good ending for the story. (If children are having problems with the concepts of story beginnings or endings, teachers might offer possible examples. Also, during read aloud time, teachers could ask children to pay particular attention to the way the stories begin and end).

A finished language experience story written by the students about a recent building of a snowman might look like this:

Our Snowman

This morning we made a snowman.
We used six stones for his mouth.
Jason put his hat on the snowman's head.
We found some twigs for his arms.
He looks cold and unhappy standing there.
If the sun keeps shining, he might melt!
We named our snowman Mister Frosty.

During the dictation phase, the teacher should try as much as possible to accept the students' words verbatim. If incorrect grammar or an unclear thought is offered, the teacher might try to rephrase the sentence by asking, "Did you mean _____?" This is usually acceptable to the child, as long as the meaning is kept intact and the teacher is not perceived as criticizing the child's dialect; in fact, this approach, sensitively used, can assist a limited English speaker to make the transition to Standard English more easily.

Read the Story Aloud

Next, the teacher and students read the story together chorally, while the teacher directs the children to read from left to right with a general sweeping motion of the hand. This reading together step has at least three distinct advantages: 1) It emphasizes the proper left to right orientation of our language; 2) it provides a multisensory experience, i.e. the children are "listening" and "looking" at the same time; and 3) it allows slower children to participate in the reading experience while automatically being "fed" the words they may have forgotten; no one fails! In the choral reading step, all new words in the story are being reinforced.

Individual Sentence Reading

While most techniques for teaching reading present the child with letters, then words, and then go from these "fragments" to whole stories, language experience does the reverse: All the children have already read the entire story; now the teacher recruits children to read each sentence and thus, the children's attention is focused on the sentence unit as part of the story. Also, more reinforcement is being provided for new individual words, as well as a review of basic sight vocabulary.

Word Framing

To further impress the new sight vocabulary into the children's memory, they are next called up to the board individually. They then follow oral directions such as being asked to point to, underline, star, etc., particular words from the story that the teacher has selected for the newest "controlled vocabulary." This is also the time when new phonic elements are introduced. For example, the teacher says, "Elvira, please come to the board and put an 'X' above the word that begins like '*st*ove' and '*st*ar' and '*st*ick.' You can find it in the second line of the story." Or "Who can put the word 'snowman' in a box three times?" Or "I see five words in our story that begin just like 'mouse.' Who would like to find them and put a circle around each one?"

Name the Story

Finding the main idea of a story or paragraph often seems to be one of the most difficult comprehension skills for most children to master. However, after much daily practice with selecting titles for language experience stories, children quickly grasp the idea of honing in on one general thought that best conveys what the story is about. Several nominations of titles for each story can be requested and then a short discussion generated about why one title does a better job of summarizing the major points in the story. For instance, the teacher might want the children to see why "Our Snowman" is a more appropriate name for the preceding language experience story than "A Cold Day" which, of course, only addresses a minor point in the story.

Specific Skill Work

After the language experience story has been written and read, the teacher now has eight or ten new vocabulary words with which to introduce new phonic elements. From "Our Snowman," for example, one might select the words "mouth," "made," "morning," "might," "melt," and "Mister" to introduce the "m" sound to the children for the first time. The following steps could be used to teach beginning sounds in this way:

   1) Put the words on the board and have the children copy them on 3x5 cards. Point out specific sounds you wish to emphasize by underlining those letters:

<u>m</u>outh	<u>M</u>ister
<u>m</u>orning	<u>m</u>elt
<u>m</u>ight	<u>m</u>ade

2) Pronounce each word for the children (or ask for volunteers to say them) and stress the sounds being presented. Ask the children what they notice about the beginning (or ending, or middle) sounds when they listen very carefully. Say them again.
3) Ask the children to look at the words as they are said again and point out how they are all the same. Repeat the words, pointing to and accenting (but not isolating) the part(s) you are introducing. Plan to have many backup examples.
4) Invite the children to verbalize what they have observed, in their own words.
5) When you feel all children have made the deduction, ask them to listen as you say more words that have the sound (e.g. "monster," "mother," "moose"). Let them think of some, too.

Similarly, long and short vowel sounds may be presented during this phase of the Language Experience Activity. Because the English language is so unpredictable, I do not suggest teaching intricate phonics rules by rote, which are often not very useful, nor are they applied by children once they have been memorized. For example, the rule "when two vowels go walking, the first does the talking" does little more than confuse a child: Consider the words "chief" and "does" and "mouth"! An alternative approach might be simply to present vowel elements in chart form, isolating consistent vowel patterns:

s	u n
r	u n
f	u n
b	u n

s n	o w
r	o w
b l	o w
f l	o w

m	i l d
w	i l d
c h	i l d

After the words are introduced in this way, the steps described for presenting beginning sounds can be followed.

To help beginning readers to remember the sounds of short vowels, a vowel chart, displayed in a place where all can see it, can be very helpful:

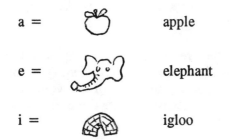

a =   apple

e =   elephant

i =   igloo

o = 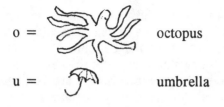   octopus

u =   umbrella

Children who speak limited English need an extra dose of multisensory teaching to get a handle on the sounds of the English language, some of which may not be in the phonology of their native language. Besides the vowel chart, the teacher may want to use "food phonics" to help the children remember the sounds. Using this technique, the teacher brings in "half an apple" to reinforce short "a"; "red jello" for "e"; an "inch of licorice" for "i"; a lollipop" for "o"; and "bubble gum" for "u". This activity has the added advantage of demonstrating to children the sounds of the vowels when they are in the middle of words, as they most frequently are.

Additionally, "action phonics" can be used to teach children beginning consonants (e.g., "m"), beginning consonant blends (e.g., "gr"), and beginning consonant digraphs (e.g., "sh"). For each of these consonants and clusters, the teacher writes a verb on a 3"x 5" card. The verb should be one that can easily be acted out. For example, the word "grab" would be the word for the blend "gr." Each child is given a word card and helped to sound out his/her word. Then each child is asked to pantomime the word on his/her card. The other children in the class must guess the action that is being acted out, tell the blend, and the sound it makes. In the previous example, the children would chorus, "grab," "gr," "grub." Thus, children for whom English is difficult begin to associate the sounds of letters with real actions—and real food, clearly providing a source of motivation.

In working with new words that children meet while doing Language Experience Stories, you may wish to help children discover certain "cues" that lead them to expect a long or a short vowel. For instance, the silent "e" at the end of a word such as "kite" consistently signals a long sound, as does a single vowel letter at the end of a word or syllable, as in "go" or "before."

Structural analysis can be presented also during this time. An example of this important skill, which involves identifying prefixes, suffixes, and root words, would be the selection of the word "unhappy" in our previous snowman story. Other words containing the same prefix would be written on the board:

unhappy
untie
unkind
uncover
unafraid
unbutton

In addition to the steps mentioned for introducing phonic elements, children would be asked to explain how the new beginning part changes the meanings of the new words, as these additions often change the words in fairly consistent ways.

Duplicate the Story

The last segment in the Language Experience Activity involves the incomparable joy of publication: each story is carefully mimeographed by the teacher and distributed to each "author." Children can then be encouraged to design a proper cover—as elaborate as they wish—to bind this story with others that will soon compile an authentic and original book.

Finally, stories should be reviewed with the children often to reinforce sight vocabulary and also because the children will be eager and proud to do so. They should also be given ample opportunities to read their books to other classes, to create taped "read alongs" for slower children, and to share their anthologies at home with their families.

Summary

When supplementing the basal reader with an Affective Reading Program, the Language Experience Approach seems a viable method for appealing to the hearts of beginning readers and making reading a very personal and exciting activity. Not only does this method allow children to select the content of what they read, but it also enables teachers to help children acquire word recognition skills and build a sight vocabulary naturally, as an integral part of their speaking, writing, and living experiences. It demands only that teachers be aware of not just what *they* think is exciting or important in the flow of daily events, but rather, of what is most significant from a child's fresh-eyed world view. To successfully teach beginning readers with the Language Experience Approach, teachers must get "down to earth" where the ant hills are. Remember: to a child, every oily mud puddle contains a glorious rainbow that is worthy of reading and writing about!

References

Ashton-Warner, S. (1959). *Spinster*. New York: Simon & Schuster.

Ashton-Warner, S. (1963). *Teacher*. New York: Bantam Books.

Hall, M. (1981). *Teaching Reading as a Language Experience*. Columbus: Merrill.

Lee, D.M. and R.V. Allen. (1963). *Learning to Read Through Experience*. New York: Appleton-Century-Crofts.

Shapiro, J. (1991). "Research Perspectives on Whole-Language." In V. Froese (ed.) *Whole-Language: Practice and Theory*. Boston: Allyn and Bacon.

Veatch, J., F. Sowicki; G. Elliott; E. Flake and J. Blakey. (1979). *Key Words to Reading: The Language Experience Approach Begins*. Columbus: Merrill.

Chapter Five

Getting Meaning from the Printed Page

We always read for some purpose—unless some sad, mad, bad schoolteacher has got hold of us.
—I. A. Richards, *How to Read a Page*

At the age of eighteen months, Jason has learned to interpret countless signs: the donning of a bib means he will soon eat; a frisky puppy leads him to expect a warm wet kiss; the pungent smell of cherry pipe tobacco suggests that Uncle David is near and may soon tickle him. The child attends to such stimuli and remembers the actual event for a long time. But various other stimuli—the whistling of a teakettle, or the slap of a newspaper on the front porch—have no associations at all for Jason yet, and he ignores and forgets them.

In general, Jason has learned to respond to certain stimuli while ignoring others, and his behavior gives us a key to the nature of "meaning." The toddler has learned to derive meaning from the uses of things, people, events—just as we do. The uses are really just their consequences for *him*, and he discriminates among the vast array of stimuli around him largely on the basis of a thing's personal significance to him. Likewise, when Jason begins to learn to read, the material must somehow have personal significance for him so that he can understand and assimilate it into part of who he is and what he knows.

For a reading program to reach the heart of Jason or any child, reading needs to become a comfortable, intimate relationship between the reader—with his or her own personal associations and experiences—and the new meanings to be gleaned from the printed page. The Language Experience Approach was presented in chapter four as one way to foster such a relationship at the very beginning reading stage. This chapter will include some other instructional approaches to help make reading become a meaningful activity.

The Directed Reading/Thinking Activity

Reading with comprehension requires more than passive attention to the written page; it requires that children actively construct meaning according to what they know of the world. The Directed Reading/Thinking Activity (Stauffer, 1969) was designed to guide children into reading in this active fashion.

The DRTA generally consists of the following teacher-guided steps:

1. Developing key vocabulary and concepts. Through drama, pantomime, brainstorming, discussion, and games, as well as careful attention to the visual aspects, new words and concepts are introduced.

2. Motivation/Connection to Prior Knowledge. To deeply comprehend, children must have sufficient background knowledge about the subject that is to be introduced. This can be provided vicariously through a discussion about the topic, bringing in pictures, a video or audio tape about the topic, or showing children some object associated with the topic. If the topic *is* familiar to students, they can be engaged in making predictions of what they think the story/article will be about from the picture, title, or after the teacher has read the first paragraph.

3. Set a purpose. The teacher should set a purpose for reading so that children's attention is focused on the most important ideas. In some cases, they may set their own purpose(s) by generating questions they have about the topic.

4. Silent or Shared Reading. Children may read silently or they may read with partners, taking turns. For increased understanding, the child who is not reading may then summarize the reader's paragraph and then the pair can switch roles. With children for whom the text is too difficult, "echo" reading may sometimes be used, especially for material that is predictable or for poetry (Wiseman, 1992). Using this technique, children simply repeat lines of text after the teacher reads them.

5. Comprehension check. Literal, predictive, and critical thinking questions can be interspersed throughout the reading of the story/article, or can be discussed in accepting, "grand conversational" tone rather than in threatening, "grand inquisition" style. Other comprehension activities are found in the next section.

6. Extended Language Activities. To enhance the feeling of the story/article, and to help the children internalize and remember it, the reading can be followed by many activities that can segue into many other curricular areas. Children can respond via journals, discussions, retelling with puppets or flannelboard characters, role plays, games, and interviews, to name just a few (The sky is the limit here!).

Facilitating Comprehension

For optimum comprehension—and enjoyment—to take place, all that a child already knows and feels about a topic needs to be brought freshly to mind before the child reads. The teacher needs somehow to bring the child's background of knowledge together with the information that will soon be encountered so that the child can best organize, comprehend, and remember it. This precursor to reading is called "the facilitating phase" of comprehension development, as nothing "new" is actually taught; rather, it sets the stage for the child to experience the most meaningful interaction with the reading material.

Though it is necessary even at the beginning stages of reading to facilitate comprehension, let's take a look at an example of how this readiness for reading phase occurs in one sixth-grade class, and later, with second-grade pupils.

Semantic Mapping

Mrs. Mohnkern wants to prepare a small group of children to read an article in *National Geographic* that, knowing the interest and reading level of these particular students, she feels they might enjoy. The story is a high adventure tale called "Alone Across the Outback" about a young woman who travels the width of Australia with four camels and a dog. The teacher hopes these pupils will come away from the reading experience with a feeling of the "flavor" of the Australian outback, as well as some real admiration for the courage of the young woman.

The first thing Mrs. Mohnkern tries to do to prepare her students to best relate to and want to read the selection is to tap the resources of experience and associations the children already have about Australia and its people: She uses a technique called "Semantic Mapping" (McNeil, 1984). First Mrs. Mohnkern writes the word "Australia" on the board and asks the students, "What do you think of when you hear this word?" The following free-association responses are classified by the teacher onto the blackboard as the students brainstorm them out loud:

kangaroo	Sydney	few people	"land down under"
wallaby	Canberra	far away	"island continent"
kookaburra		very large	
koala bear			

The children are then asked to label the categories of the items in each column. After some discussion, the columns are named "Animals Found in Australia," "Cities in Australia," "Facts about Australia," and

"Nicknames of Australia." By asking her students to label the columns, Mrs. Mohnkern has provided her students with a framework for their present knowledge of Australia, to be augmented later as new understandings emerge from the reading.

Student Initiated Questions

Next, the students are asked to look at the title of the article and the accompanying picture of the author nuzzling one of the camels and offering him food from a pail. Mrs. Mohnkern asks the children, "What would you like to know about this young woman after looking at the title and the picture?" The responses go something like this:

"What is an 'outback'?"
"What did the woman eat?"
"Why did the girl go alone?"
"How many miles did she travel?"
"Did she meet anyone along the way?"
"How long did the trip take?"
"Why did she take camels and not a horse?"
"Did she ever feel like turning back?"
                              (Singer, 1978)

After introducing some new (and exotic!) vocabulary that will soon be met in the article, the teacher asks her pupils to read the article to find the answers to the questions they have asked. Thus armed with their self-selected purposes for reading, the students intently "devour" the article. Later, they eagerly add their new findings about Australia to the chart on the blackboard.

Story Grammar

In another classroom, Mr. Vidler facilitates comprehension in a different way for his second-grade pupils, who mainly seem to enjoy fictional stories or narrative. He guides them toward maximum comprehension of this genre by teaching pupils the components that one can expect to find in a well-crafted story in a fun way. This approach is called "story grammar," or the use of a structure to enhance the comprehension of stories that are to be read (Fitzgerald and Spiegel, 1983). Story grammar also provides a framework for children's creative ideas and thus motivates them to write.

Mr. Vidler uses the following steps to facilitate comprehension through the use of story grammar:

1) Read the children a well-formed short story, pointing out the particular elements that are usually found in a short story (e.g. setting, main characters, key episode, result, original story ending).

2) Write a story with the group of children, using the blackboard or overhead transparency. You provide the structure, but have the children fill in the blanks:

Example

Once upon a time in _____, there lived a _____ .
                    where (setting)   (character)
(S)he was very _____ and always liked to _____ .
              (description)   (favorite activity)
One day early in the morning (character) decided to try something new. (S)he wanted very much to _____ so (s)he _____ .
                                        (key episode)   (description)
(S)he tried and tried, and finally _____ . (Character)
                                        (result)
learned _____ .
         (original ending)

Encourage children to volunteer ideas for the individual blanks using words, phrases, or even paragraphs, as they wish.

3) When the story is completed, allow one child to read the whole story aloud.

4) Give the children a framework to use so that they can write their own personal stories. The teacher may wish to hold a session of brainstorming with the whole class first, in order to inspire the children and help them to get started. For example, they may generate a host of ideas for a main character: a skinny elephant, a near-sighted scientist, an invisible shark, etc.

Ultimately, Mr. Vidler shows the children the connection between their student-written attempts and reading professionally-written stories. During student-teacher conferences, the parts of the story just read are casually pointed out ("Look, Mr. Vidler! Dr. Seuss did it *right*!"). Similarly, the teacher calls children's attention to story structure in reading aloud to them.

K-W-L

The K-W-L strategy is effective because it encourages children to bring to the surface all they know about a topic, motivates them to ask questions about the topic, and then helps them to use the text to discover the answers to their own questions (Carr & Ogle, 1987). The

"K" represents all the information that children brainstorm about what they know (or think they know) about a topic and each idea is written on a chart or board before the reading. The "W" stands for what children want to know about the topic, and these questions are written in a second column on the chart of board. These questions set the purpose for the children's reading. Finally, the "L" represents what the children learned about the topic after reading the text; this section comprises the third column on the chart and is completed after the reading. Also after the reading, children discuss what they have learned and answer their own questions. They also either confirm or deny the statements in the "K" (know) column. This procedure works especially well with expository, or content area, material.

Direct Instruction in Comprehension

Children at some time may need teacher-directed help with certain comprehension skills so that they can understand and appreciate what they are reading more fully. The goal of this teacher-directed assistance is to have a positive effect on children's thinking ability as they move through the text.

Experience-Text-Relationship Method

When a specific comprehension skill weakness has been identified through the student-teacher conference, the teacher may want to pull an *ad hoc* group together to "walk them through" the skill using an Experience-Text-Relationship Method (ETR) (Au, 1979). Use of this discussion method helps the teachers to pinpoint and remediate comprehension problems by allowing them to model the kinds of thinking that typify adequate comprehension. The three steps in ETR include:

1. Experience Sequence. This stage is similar to facilitation, where background for the new material is taught.

2. Text Sequence. In this stage, the teacher attempts to determine what sense the pupil is getting from the text by stopping to ask questions and talk about what is happening every paragraph or so. When necessary, the teacher clarifies misunderstandings.

3. Relationship Sequence. After the story has been read, the teacher tries to incorporate new learning with what was originally brought to the text from the pupil's own personal feelings and experiences.

In the following example, a group of three fourth-grade students go through ETR. These children have lately been reading all the fairy tales they could find and have enjoyed dramatizing them for the rest of the class. Presently, they have selected a tale called "The Practical Princess" about a very unorthodox princess with a good deal of common sense. Miss Hall, concerned that the author's clever use of satire may not be understood by the children, walks them through the story like this:

1. Experience Sequence

Miss Hall: Do any of you know what it means to be "practical"? Can you give me an example of something you or someone else has ever done that was especially "practical"?

Janet: Well, once we asked my mother if she wanted a mink coat for her birthday. She said she would rather have a microwave because it would be more "practical" for her.

Miss Hall: That's a *great* example! Maybe it's more practical for her to have a microwave because she would use it more—it would be more sensible for her. Now I'd like us to read a story about a princess who is not like some of the princesses you may already have read about. She is constantly using her head to get out of bad situations. Let's find out what she does that makes her seem so "practical" . .

*****

2. Text Sequence

As the children read several paragraphs at a time, Miss Hall stops them periodically to discuss the text. By probing their thinking as they are reading, she tries to clear up misunderstandings and shows them how to think through certain confusing points:

Miss Hall: Why does the princess say to the dragon that he only wants to marry her because he's a "snob"?

Craig: She doesn't want to marry a dragon. She's probably waiting for Prince Charming! (other laugh)

Miss Hall: That's what happens in lots of stories, isn't it, Craig? But I think this princess said it for another reason. Does the dragon really love the princess, do you think?

Kristen: No—he just thinks he has to marry a princess because princesses are special. That's why she calls the dragon a snob.

Miss Hall: I think you're right, Kristen. It doesn't matter at all what she's like as long as she's a princess. How do you feel about this dragon's thinking?

*****

3. Relationship Sequence

Thus having cleared up several confusions similar to the one cited in the text sequence, Miss Hall is confident the children have gained a fuller appreciation of the tale. She is now ready to contrast the story with the students' prior experiences:

Miss Hall: Have you ever known anyone who used their head to get out of bad experiences the way Princess Bedelia did?

Kristen: Only in *Raiders of the Lost Ark*. Princesses usually don't use their heads. It's neat the way she did, though. She could have just married the dragon because she was supposed to.

Miss Hall: Yes—that's what we might have expected from other fairy tales. How did you like how she kept from marrying the dragon?

Craig: It was great. She got him to come out of the cave by telling him to get her and then she blew him up. That's like how I trick my dog to get him to take a bath. He hides under the bed when he sees the towel, so I bribe him out with a dog biscuit!

Janet: It sounds like you use *your* common sense to get your dog into the bathtub!

Craig: Yeah—I guess I'm "practical" sometimes too, right?

*****

What, Why, How, When Procedure

Another method for the direct teaching of specific comprehension skills involves giving children a detailed explanation about the particular skill and then modeling that skill. The teacher discusses with the child:
1) *What* the comprehension skill is;
2) *Why* it is important for the child to learn;
3) *How* to use the strategy;
4) *When* the comprehension skill should be used.
(Baumann and Schmitt, 1986)

Let's see how this procedure is used in Mrs. Morgan's student-teacher conference with the third-grader, Ryan. Mrs. Morgan has talked to the whole class about finding main ideas—or topic sentences—in Social Studies material by looking for repeated words. Now Mrs. Morgan wants to prepare Ryan to better understand a paragraph in which several pronoun referrals are made:

1. What. "Yesterday in Social Studies we discussed the fact that sometimes a writer repeats words, and that helps you to find the main idea in a paragraph. We called the main idea the 'topic sentence,' remember? Sometimes instead of repeating the same word over and over, the author will use a word like 'he' or 'she' or 'it.' These words, or 'pronouns,' take the place of words so that the author doesn't have to keep using the same words over and over again."

2. Why. "When the authors use pronouns instead of using the same words over and over again, it's easy to get confused about who or what the pronoun is meaning. But if you can figure out who or what the pronoun is referring to, it will help you to find and remember the main idea of the paragraph."

3. How. To find the main idea of the paragraph when many pronouns are used try using these steps: (these are written down so the child can refer to them)

a) See if any words are repeated. Underline them once.

b) Underline the pronouns twice.

c) Try to decide which words the pronouns are replacing.

d) When you have figured out which words most of the pronouns are replacing, you will probably have found the main idea of the paragraph.

"Let's look at this paragraph from your book and see how we could use the pronouns to help us find the main idea."

The Kookaburra lives in Australia. It lives in the forest in small groups. Kookaburras are very friendly. They will accept food from people. Sometimes they even tap on windows to be fed. Kookaburras eat insects, crabs, fish and small birds. They are also quite famous as snake killers.

"Now let's look at our steps. Step one tells you to see if any words are repeated. As I read it again, I see that one word is repeated three times—Kookaburra. So I underline all the 'Kookaburras.'"

"Step two says to underline all the pronouns. Let's see—I can find one 'it' and three 'theys.'"

"Now in step three we are asked to figure out exactly who or what the pronouns are replacing. 'It lives in the forest.' It has to mean the Kookaburra. 'They will accept food from people . . . they even tap on windows to be fed . . . They are famous as snake killers.' These three words, all the same pronouns, are also talking about the Kookaburra.

"The last step says we should know what the main idea is when we have found out what all the pronouns are referring to. They were all used to replace the Kookaburra, so I guess the topic must be 'The Kookaburra.' What do you think?"

4. When. "One last thing about using pronouns to find the main idea, Ryan. The paragraph you just read was 'informational writing'—that is, it told you facts, or information about the Kookaburra. But you can also use this skill with stories, not so much to find the main idea, but to keep track of *who* or *what* the author is talking about in each paragraph."

Monitoring Cards

The Monitoring Cards approach for the enhancement of reading comprehension is especially suited to the independent nature of the Affective Reading Program. This program encourages students to monitor their *own* comprehension while they read their self-selected material. The monitoring should not be used all the time, as its overuse may become a burdensome routine, but a bit of practice with this "novelty" approach can help children to become better evaluators of their own reading.

The student is given nine small cards with the following information on them:
1) Click — "I understand."
2) Clunk — "I don't understand."
3) Read on.
4) Reread the sentence.
5) Go back and reread the paragraph.
6) Look in the glossary or dictionary.
7) Ask someone.
8) What did it say? (to check comprehension at the paragraph level)
9) What do I remember? (to check comprehension at the page level)

(Babbs, 1984)

As the students read, they are told to "think about their thinking" and check their response to each sentence they are reading. For example, if the student feels he or she understands the sentence being read, (s)he raises the "Number 1 Click—I understand" card and goes on to the next sentence. If, however, the "Number 2" Clunk card is raised, the student must then try to solve the comprehension problem by using one of the 3 through 7 cards, which offer strategies for the child to use when his or her own lack of understanding has become evident.

Next, a further self-check on comprehension is provided by the Number 8 card—"What did it say?"—which is raised after the whole paragraph has been read. If the child is not satisfied that (s)he can remember what the paragraph said, (s)he goes back and rereads the paragraph.

Finally, after each page of the material has been read the student raises the Number 9 card that asks "What do I remember?" The student must then try to recall and summarize the information on the whole page. Failing this, the student rereads the page using the "What did it say?" card again after each paragraph.

Summary

One of the goals of the Affective Reading Program is to make reading a satisfying relationship between the reader and the material he or she has chosen to read. Therefore, it is often necessary to help children freshly crystallize their ideas, associations and experiences about a subject before they read. This facilitating stage, with the teacher's gentle guidance, allows children to get the fullest personal enjoyment and appreciation from the text. This personal significance is the key to the nature of meaning.

With the use of the Semantic Map, existing background is tapped and children become ready to organize and comprehend new information. Also, children can set their own purposes for reading, and thus learn to guide their comprehension, through Student-Initiated Questions that are carefully elicited by the teacher. A third approach, Story Grammar, can help children to organize and comprehend narratives by leading them to understand what to expect when they read stories. These three approaches to facilitating comprehension assure greater interaction between the reader and text.

More direct methods of teaching comprehension are often needed when certain deficits in understanding text are getting in the way of maximum appreciation. When problems are noted through student-teacher conferences or in other reading situations, several direct methods can often clear up the problems. The Experience-Text-Relationship Method pinpoints specific misunderstandings as they occur and helps children to see another way to look at the text. The What, Why, How, When Procedure lets the teacher directly model how to use a certain comprehension strategy. Finally, Monitoring Cards can be used on occasion to encourage children to think about and evaluate their own thinking.

The methods just described for enhancing a child's comprehension all have one thing in common: each recognizes that reading is "responding." The response may be at the surface level of "calling" the word, but the Affective Teacher hopes it will not stop there. The response may be at the somewhat deeper level of understanding the explicit meaning of the sentence, paragraph, or passage. Still, the Affective Teacher is not satisfied. Such a teacher strives to get children on the third level of reading—going beyond the facts to the discovery of new and personal meaning with fresh and creative images and thoughts. So, of course, the Affective Teacher smiles when Kristen muses ". . . it was so brave of the Princess not to marry the dragon. She would probably prefer an astronaut who thinks for himself and is just as courageous as she is. In fact, maybe she'll decide to stop being a princess and become an astronaut herself!"

References

Au, K.H. (1979). "Using the Experience-Text-Relationship Method with Minority Children." *The Reading Teacher* 32, no. 6, March: 677-679.

Babbs, P.J. (1984). "Monitoring Cards Can Help Improve Comprehension." *The Reading Teacher* 38, no. 2, November: 200-204.

Baumann, J.F., and M.C. Schmitt. (1986). "The What, Why, How and When of Comprehension Instruction." *The Reading Teacher* 39, no. 7, March: 640-645.

Carr, E., and D. Ogle. (1987). K-W-L Plus: "A Strategy for Comprehension and Summarization." *Journal of Reading*, 30 (7), 626-631.

Davidson, R. (1978). "Alone Across the Outback." *National Geographic* 153, no. 5, May: 581-611.

Fitzgerald, J., and D.L. Spiegel. (1983). "Enhancing Children's Reading Comprehension Through Instruction in Narrative Structure." *Journal of Reading Behavior* 15, no. 2, March: 1017.

McNeil, J.D. (1984). *Reading Comprehension: New Directions for Classroom Practice*. Glenview, IL: Scott, Foresman.

Richards, I.A. (1984). *How to Read a Page*. New York: W.W. Norton.

Singer, H. (1978). "Active Comprehension." *The Reading Teacher* 31, no. 8, May: 901-908.

Stauffer, R.G. (1969). *Directing Reading Maturity as a Cognitive Process*. New York: Harper & Row.

Williams, J. (1978). "The Practical Princess," from *The Practical Princess and Other Liberating Fairy Tales*. New York: Scholastic Book Services.

Wiseman D.L. (1992). *Learning to Read with Literature*. Boston: Allyn and Bacon.

Chapter Six

Reading and Writing Poetry

Tell me where is fancy bred
Or in the heart, or in the head?
How begot, how nourished?
    —William Shakespeare,
    The Merchant of Venice

Poetry, by its very nature, is an obvious "must" in an Affective Reading Program. A poem, after all, concerns *feeling*. Emotion is at the core of most poetry; poems are direct appeals to the heart rather than the head. Children enjoy being able to "tune in" to the poetically represented emotions of joy, anger, love, fear, or sadness because they, too, have experienced them.

Poetic thoughts are a child's natural thoughts—a child for whom life is incredibly new and full of intense flavor and color. Because their acquaintance with language is relatively new also, children's use of it tends to be fresh and original. Often, their expression is *so* vivid and rhythmic that it just naturally makes interesting poetry. To a child poetry is . . . a rolling green lawn that just got its hair cut . . . friendly stars that wink at you . . . earth worms taking a bath in a mud puddle, or dandelions gaily shampooing their blond hair. . .

Personally, I did not always feel absolutely positive about poetry. As a child, I had many fine teachers who loved poetry and shared that enthusiasm with me as they indulged my fanciful poetic attempts. During those years, I had no qualms about considering myself a "poet." But I can recall the exact moment when my positive perception of poetry was almost (but not *quite*) shaken beyond repair. In my eighth grade English class we were explicating the lovely poem "Stopping by Woods on a Snowy Evening." In it, Frost presents a poignant scene with an old man and his little horse out near a country woods after a fresh snowfall. It seems to be the deepest heart of winter just as it begins to get dark. While reading the poem, I could hear the jingle of the bells on the horse's reins; I could see his long eyelashes all covered with snow, and I could feel the force with which he shakes his little head. I *knew* the absolute peacefulness of the scene, for I had been there. Most of us have.

"What is this poem about, Nancy?" the teacher asks. So I verbally repaint the picture for her.

"No, that's not right. You missed the point. Frost is referring to the old man's death wish. 'And miles to go before I sleep; and miles to go before I sleep.' The man clearly is wishing to die."

A *death* wish?? I stare at her dully. I don't buy it, but she must know. . .

(Aside: Much, much later, I find that Frost is on *my* side. When told of this once common explication of his poem, Frost responded, "It doesn't please me to have it flavored so.")

Similarly, we can inspire children to express their own personal, whimsical thoughts through poetry, and respect their own interpretations. Or, on the other hand, we can systematically turn children off entirely by presenting poetry as a very precise and rigid form of writing that is simply much too esoteric for most children's uncomplicated view of the world. In this chapter we will look at some ways to inspire children to write poetry.

Listening to Poetry

Children should hear poetry read aloud from the very beginning of their learning to read experience. They begin to appreciate poetry by listening to the rhythm, beat, repeating patterns, and the sounds of the words. It is my suggestion that the teacher first select poems that he or she feels very close to in order to train the "inner ear" of children to listen. Children will first begin to respond to what "sounds" good to them without knowing (or caring) why; this is exactly the natural, inner ear intuition which we need to encourage and nurture.

Heller (1991) suggests that poetry be read aloud to children every single day so that they begin to tune in to its rhythm, repetition, and music-like qualities that are so close to a child's heart. She states that the poetic selections can be rhymed, unrhymed, nonsense verse, lyrical, or ballad, but that the nature of the poetry must have some innate, immediate appeal to the children. She further warns teachers against selecting poems that are beyond the developmental level of the children so that the meaning must be laboriously explained to them. Such practices have led to a lasting resistance to poetry for far too many children.

The range of poems selected to read to the class may be of any variety: classic poetry, such as Blake's "The Tyger," poems written especially for children, such as the collections of Shel Silverstein or John Ciardi; or any poems fondly remembered from the teacher's experience. After a while, the children may want to contribute poems that they have "discovered." After listening to the poems, children may be asked to react by asking and answering open-ended questions, e.g. "Does the scene in this poem remind you of any place you have ever been? Tell us about it." They might be encouraged to respond through an art form, by dramatizing how the poem makes them feel, or just by orally sharing intimate reactions or impressions. Again—there is no "right" or "wrong" answer, only personal responses which are *always* valid. Any poem read aloud is then, of course, prominently displayed in the classroom, or duplicated, for interested individuals to read by themselves when and if they wish. The seeds are now planted.

Because poetry is such a special kind of writing, it also lends itself to some unique methods of presenting it in creative ways:

1) Poems can be introduced and then shared chorally; students get a chance to feel the basic rhythm of the poem without experiencing frustration if they cannot immediately decode every word. Blake's "The Tyger" is perfect for this approach.

2) Poems can be acted out in groups. After the poem has been written on the chalkboard and read aloud, students can be divided into small groups to discuss what the poem is saying to them, and then encouraged to act out their impressions for the rest of the class. The groups' contrasting interpretations can later be discussed and appreciated by all.

3) Poems can be disassembled and then reassembled. After its presentation, a poem can be placed on strips of paper and passed out to individuals or groups of students. They can then reassemble the poem in front of the class and recite their lines orally.

4) Special "mood" poems can be read to the class, and actions and sound effects added to enhance the particular feelings evoked by the poem. For example, Poe's "The Bells" could be accompanied by a xylophone or water-filled glasses, or "The Song of Hiawatha" might include simulated drum beats. Sound effects would, of course, be provided by eager volunteers (Smith, 1975).

Listening to Students' Poetry

Listening to and appreciating poetry is one thing; writing it is quite another. However, the highest possible appreciation occurs only after *both* have been experienced. I have found that an ideal way to initially encourage children to create their own poetry is to begin by reading them poems other children have written. As compared with Blake's "Tyger" or other classic poetry, a child's poem is filled with interesting yet singularly childlike thoughts such as these:

Gray

Gray is the color of a mist.
Gray is the sound a snake has hissed.
Gray are my shoes;
And gray is a sickness you want to lose.
Gray is someone's gray watch band;
Gray is the fog or half-burned log.
Gray is a sea gull,
And gray is a color is thin and dull.

Nancy, Grade 4

Reading poems like "Gray" or other children's poems often provokes a reaction like this: "Oh, wow—I could do as well as that, or maybe even *better*!" The teachers' personal collections of their students' poetry are perhaps the best source of poems for the purpose of "inspiring," but for variety, the following books can furnish an interesting selection of children's poetry that can be read aloud by the teacher or individual students:

First Voices by Geoffrey Summerfield
Children and Poets by Susan Pulsifer
Wishes, Lies and Dreams by Kenneth Koch

Introducing Poem Ideas

The next phase in creating poets is twofold. It involves 1) presenting a simple "poem idea," and then 2) using that idea to jointly compose a poem together using the chalkboard or overhead projector.

The rationale for the poem idea is that it gives the children something concrete to work with. Although a suggestion to "write a poem about spring" would seem open-ended enough to allow each child to freely express his or her individuality, often children are "stumped" by such an assignment. "I don't know where to begin!" is the frequent lament. The ideas are buried somewhere but they just aren't sure how to tap them. Koch (1970) offers several poem ideas that are provocative to children and also provide the structure to help them get started:

1) "I wish..." (All lines begin like this.)
    Example
    I wish I could ride my bike all night long;
    I wish I had a little sister instead of a big brother;
    I wish my whole house was made of chocolate;
    I wish I was the smartest kid in the school;
    And I wish all my wishes would come true!

                                        Traci, Grade 3

2) "I dream..." (All lines begin with this. For variation, each line
    may also contain a color, a famous person, and a place, etc.)
    Example
    I dream I dance with President Clinton on a blue green island;
    I dream Michael Jackson flies me to Chicago in a blue jet;
    I dream Mr. T chases my black cat to California,
    And I dream I wake up in my pretty pink bedroom.

                                        Nellie, Grade 3

3) "I was...
    "I became...
    "Now I'm..." (The triplets begin with this pattern. Each triplet
    can be connected or not, as the child wishes.)
    Example
    I was born tiny and weak;
    I became rich and muscular and strong;
    Now I'm in Spain taking my time!

    I was once very, very scared.
    I became a black belt in karate.
    Now I'm not afraid of anything!

                                        Danny, Grade 3

4) "Red is as red as..." (Each line may begin with the same color,
    or each line with a different color.)
    Example
    Red is as red as a strawberry day.
    Red is as red as popsicle juice.
    Red is anger; red is so brave;
    Red is the red of a fiery feeling,
    And red is the balloon swallowed up by the sky.

                                        Julie, Grade 3

5) "Give me..." (Each line begins this way; for variety, each line
might include an animal and a number, etc.)
Example
Give me a hot meal and a warm bed.
Give me a little dog that follows me everywhere.
Give me one whole summer without rain
And let me see what I can do.

Andrew, Grade 3

When a variety of these poem ideas have been explored, other
more complex poetic forms can also be introduced. For example, the
cinquain consists of:

Line 1 — one word (usually the title)
Line 2 — two words (describing the title)
Line 3 — three words (action describing the title)
Line 4 — four words (feelings describing the title)
Line 5 — one word (referring back to the title)

Twister
Blowing hard
Rushes, swishes, screams
Circling, pulling, scaring, lifting
Tornado.

Joshua, Grade 3

A literacy scaffold, or temporary structure, can be a kind of
formula for writing a poem by imitating an existing poem. In the
following poem by a fourth-grade class (with the help of a dictionary)
all words begin with the letter "t". There are ten adjectives and the
ending couplet is a mirror image of the beginning couplet (Cecil, 1993):

Turtles
Turtles are timid,
Turtles are tired.
Tactful, tacky,
Tardy, tough.
Testy, tasteful,
Terrified, trusting.
Turtles are tired,
Turtles are timid.

Hoa, Grade 4

Writing a Group Poem

To write a group poem, the teacher simply presents a poem idea and lets children volunteer lines that are then written on the board by the teacher, or in the upper grades, by the author of the line. The actual writing of the poem can be preceded by a "brainstorming" session in the case of the cinquain or haiku. For example, if the group has decided to write a haiku on "monsters," words that they associate with monsters can be first written on the board to arouse general enthusiasm about the topic and furnish ideas.

The following is an illustration of a class collaboration composed by a group of third graders that I taught in the U.S. Virgin Islands. As it was in the initial stages of their poetic attempts, the poem idea was simple: Each line might begin with "I wish" and also contain a color, a place, and a cartoon character.

> I wish I had a long white coat like Wonder Woman in Barbados;
> I wish I was as pink as Pink Panther in Puerto Rico;
> I wish I had a gold and silver vest like Mighty Mouse in Morocco;
> I wish I lived in a great big red house in England when I visit Goldie Gold;
> I wish I had Tarzan's brown skin when he swings in those trees in Tortola;
> And mostly I wish I could wear lipstick and have a red smile like Snowwhite in Guadalupe.

When each "Magnum Opus" has been completed (no magic number of lines; just group consensus), it is read by a teacher or volunteer, and then chorally (with gusto) by the children. Later, it is duplicated so that each child can begin to collect poems for his or her own poetry booklet.

After such a successful joint effort and many verbal "pats on the back," children are then eager to try their *own* hands at becoming poets.

Some Guidelines for Creating Poets

The next poetry session will be met with (I guarantee) a most positive response. You will need only to introduce an idea, perhaps brainstorm a few ideas, and then let the students begin. *Your* function now is to praise, encourage, and "feed" your students words that they now want to know how to spell. The following suggestions may also be helpful:

1) Do *NOT* insist that students meticulously adhere to the poem's "rules"; remember, the purpose of the poem idea is *only* to stimulate them and to help them start writing. If they don't need the structure and feel comfortable with "free verse," that should be acceptable. This point should be made to the class, as children can be rigid about rules and may tend to criticize others who haven't followed them exactly.

2) Each and every poem and thought has value—there is no right or wrong. You may only need, at times, to help a child to elaborate on his own basic message by prompting, "That's a wonderful thought, but can you tell me even *more* about that pink clown?"

3) Separate the creative and editing processes. Let the children hastily jot down their ideas and you respond to those ideas. Then, in a totally different session (perhaps during "language arts") help them to transform the rough draft into a final, mechanically perfect copy. Motivate them to attend to the punctuation, spelling, and handwriting by providing opportunities for them to display their poems on the bulletin board, on the walls in the hall, or in the school or local paper.

4) Help children to avoid using the cliches they think adults want to hear by explaining that they should be as "silly" or "crazy" as they want to in their poems: "blue is as blue as the sun's breath" versus the hackneyed "blue is as blue as the sky" can then surface.

5) Try to convince students that poetry does *not* necessarily have to rhyme. Perhaps it is the very early influence of nursery rhymes, or maybe it's just that rhymes are intuitively pleasing to them; but children often expend much mental energy contriving a rhyme scheme, too often at the expense of what they really wanted to say.

A Poetry Reading

A poetry reading can be a rewarding extension of children's involvement with poetry reading and writing in the classroom (Shapiro, 1990). For this event, children can elect to read a favorite poem they have read, or one they have penned, individually, with a partner, or they may arrange a choral reading of their selection. Children may be encouraged to either read or memorize their poem, whichever seems most comfortable to them. Poems can be practiced by reading them aloud in front of a mirror, in front of a few chosen classmates, or by reading them privately into a tape recorder. When children feel ready to "perform" their selections, they can decide how to "stage" their poetry reading using appropriate props, music, and/or actions to enhance the feeling of each poem. The teacher can consult with each child to offer helpful suggestions or comments.

The culminating poetry reading can be a gala evening affair, with parents and community members invited via elaborate child-written invitations, or it could be a more casual event, requiring only another class or several staff members acting as an audience to lend their appreciation and applause.

An attractive class book of the chosen poetry selections will assure lasting memories of the poetry reading. Likewise, video-taping of the event can immortalize it while also allowing children to critique their own performances in readiness for future poetry readings.

Summary

The bottom line is that poetry just makes good sense in an Affective Reading Program because of the unique way it "opens a child up":

> . . . [T]he educational advantage of a creative, intellectual, and emotional activity which children enjoy are clear. Writing poetry makes children *feel* happy, capable, and creative. It makes them feel open to understanding and appreciating what others have written. It makes them, as budding "poets," feel close to poetry. It even makes them want to know how to spell and say things correctly. Of all these advantages, the main one is how writing poetry makes children FEEL—creative, original, responsive, sensitive, yet in command. (Koch, 1970)

A case in point is how it made Roger feel. Roger, a twelve-year-old boy who had never particularly distinguished himself, became obsessed with writing poetry. Labeled "learning disabled," he never had done well in school and no one seemed to expect much from him. One day, armed with a typewriter and a poem idea ("green is as green as...") Roger typed out such a wonderful poem that his teacher could not stop herself from gushing profusely. The poem was immediately published in the school and later the local paper. Roger's new prestige as "poet" bolstered his self-esteem, and his attitude toward school significantly improved. This is Roger's poem:

> Green is as green as someone's lost ship.
> Green is the way of the sea;
> Green is the green of all oaks in the forest.
> Green is the green of my arrow through space,
> And green is the green that abandoned the desert.

Though Roger's poem is unique, Roger's story isn't. I am convinced there are many children out there whose hearts and talents can be reached by poetry in a very special and emotional way.

References

Cecil, N.L. and P. Lauritzen. (1993). *Literacy and the Arts: Alternative Ways of Knowing*. White Plains, NY: Longman.

Ciardi, J. (1985). *Doodle Soup*, ill. by Merle Nacht. Boston: Houghton Mifflin.

Craig, H., ed. (1961). *The Complete Works of Shakespeare*. Chicago: Scott, Foresman.

Heller, M.F. (1991). *Reading-Writing Connections: From Theory to Practice*. White Plains, NY: Longman.

Keynes, G., ed. (1966). *The Complete Writings of William Blake*. London: Oxford University Press.

Koch, K. (1970). *Wishes, Lies and Dreams*. New York: Chelsea House.

Lathem, E.C., ed. (1967). *The Poetry of Robert Frost*. New York: Rinehart and Winston.

Longfellow, H.W. (1975). *The Poetical Works of Longfellow*. Boston: Houghton Mifflin.

Mabbott, T.O., ed. (1969). *Collected Works of Edgar Allen Poe*. Cambridge: Belknap, Harvard University Press.

McCord, D. (1970). *For Me to Say*. Boston: Little, Brown.

Pulsifer, S. (1963). *Children Are Poets*. Cambridge, Mass.: Dresser, Chapman and Grimes.

Shapiro, S. (1990). "Beyond the Anthology: Poetry Readings in the Classroom." In N.L. Cecil (ed.) *Literacy in the 90s: Selected Readings in the Language Arts*. Dubuque, IA: Kendall/Hunt.

Silverstein, S. (1981). *A Light in the Attic*. New York: Harper & Row.

Smith, J. (1975). *Creative Teaching of Reading in the Elementary School*. Boston: Allyn and Bacon.

Summerfield, G., ed. (1970). *First Voices*. New York: Random House.

Chapter Seven
Reading Through Creative Drama

Once upon a time, when children gave a play they
would dress up like bunnies and carrots and line up in
front of the P.T.A. Often they forgot their lines or
couldn't be heard beyond the third row. But everyone
was pleased, anyway.

— Sandra Sanders, *Creating
Plays with Children*

No reading program that considers motivation a top priority could
be complete without including the magic of drama, the ultimate avenue
for displaying feelings and emotions. Brian Way, British educator and
author of *Development Through Drama*, offers that, "Drama transcends
information and makes [reading] a living experience significant to the
heart and soul as well as to the mind . . .," a natural adjunct to an
Affective Reading Program.

Drama can become a way to elevate reading to the status of an
exciting performing art. To a child, drama is as natural as singing,
dancing, or skipping rope. Drama is simply 'play' which offers the
additional opportunity for a child to participate in sharing intimate
moments of oral and visual expression.

When one class of fifth-grade students was asked to evaluate its
drama program, responses such as these were offered:

"We write down our ideas just like playwrights do, and then we get
to act out what's in our minds. It's kind of like magic."

"[Drama] helped me learn new words and taught me to talk like all
kinds of different people and animals."

"I learned to do things I didn't know I could do . . . I felt like an
old person because you all treated me like one, and I even made people
laugh."

Their experiences with drama had obviously broadened the word banks of these children, but also went a long way toward helping them to feel more positive toward themselves and the others in the class.

Drama has some even more compelling qualities that can make it an ideal vehicle through which to reach a wide spectrum of culturally and linguistically diverse children who too often skirt the fringes of more traditional literacy activities. A committee sponsored by the National Endowment for the Arts recently concluded that:

- drama offers a creative and psychological balance to more academic instruction;
- drama is a magical experience that offers a playful and universal way to observe reality;
- drama is respectful of childhood in that it showcases a sense of pretending and wonder;
- drama enhances ability in all academic areas by making children of all linguistic and cultural groups better able to think and conceptualize (Corathers, 1991).

The goal of the drama component in an Affective Reading Program is to have children eventually write their own plays and thus, as in the language experience approach, bring to life words, feelings and ideas that have great personal significance to them. Writing plays, however, demands some experience with the play as a unique form of expression. It is often helpful, therefore, to "work students up" to the goal of actually writing plays. To minimize frustration, the drama program can be introduced in three phases: first, favorite stories are adapted into simple sketches by the teacher. Stories with much dialogue lend themselves readily to such adaptations. Second, stories shared and favorably received in the Read Aloud time are recalled, blocked, and turned into short plays by the students. Finally, with this background of script reading and working out of scenes, students are ready to write their own plays.

Introducing the Sketch

The first plays the students encounter may be simple sketches adapted by the teacher from stories with which the students are all familiar. The advantage of a teacher-made script over a commercial script is that the teacher can truly tailor the roles to the students' personalities and also contrive the number of characters to equal the number of students in the class. "Goldilocks and the Three Bears," for example, might suddenly include a narrator, various other animals encountered along the path to the three bears' house, as well as the "extended family" of the three bears:

"I don't remember anybody named 'Aunt Mildred Bear' in *Goldilocks and the Three Bears!*" remarks a slightly perplexed third-grader, but he readily accepts the explanation that, "Perhaps the author forgot to include this fine bear in the original story written long ago, but *we* can include her." The truth, of course, is that many new characters must be "invented" so that *all* students have a chance to perform. For the ultimate in attention and practice in listening skills, the teacher must also make sure that the number of lines is evenly distributed, so that no child has long idle stretches in which to let his or her mind wander. In a typical half-hour sketch, for example, each child might have five or six lines, even if a couple are only rejoinders ("me, too!") to keep everyone actively involved.

Though the most democratic method of matching roles to actors and actresses would be by popular vote, it is probably wiser at first for the teacher to make these casting decisions. Children tend to vote for their friends, or for the child who "looks the part." Consequently, much fine raw talent lurking in the plainest of Janes or Jims is often overlooked. By having the teacher initially assign parts appropriate to children's personalities and potentials, latent abilities are allowed to flourish. These talents are on display to the child's peers to recognize and appreciate—perhaps for the first time.

Before the first reading of scripts, character names and new words to be encountered can be written on the chalk board and discussed to avoid as much frustration with the sight reading as possible. Because the story is already familiar, this is not usually a problem. The students then go over each page until the reading is fluent. The play reading, quite naturally, becomes one of the few points in the reading program where children can be easily motivated to read and reread until fluency is achieved; it vies with wide recreational reading as an activity that best provides the practice needed to make decoding "automatic."

After the script can be read easily by all cast members, students are asked to memorize a couple of pages of script each day. Children are assisted in discovering the method that works best for them: Some feel comfortable reading lines over and over aloud; others write them down, saying each word as they do so; still others like to have a friend or family member "cue them in" with preceding lines.

Finally, when the scripts are committed to memory, inflections and actions appropriate to the story line are discussed, and different interpretations tried out by the students and teachers. Note: A key element in the success of the drama adventure is the willingness of the teacher(s) to believe and participate in the "coming to life" of the sketch along with the children.

Although all dramatic enterprises require an audience, these first primitive sketches don't necessarily need a proper stage, extensive props, and scenery; as a matter of fact, a "propless playlet" has the advantage of increasing the child's ability to imagine, and can easily be brought from classroom to classroom. This way, students are not overwhelmed by the large crowds, nor must they shout to be heard, for their first dramatic efforts.

The following suggestions may be helpful in making the first dramatic attempts more manageable:

1) Forget using make-up unless you have several parent volunteers. It is distracting and uncomfortable for the students and requires extra time and effort for the teacher, when what is really called for is simplicity. Better to refine the particular role by discussing appropriate character development.

2) Help students understand their role by suggesting popular models to emulate. For example, the teacher could ask, "How would Elmer Fudd say this?" or "How would Michael Jackson react in this situation?"

3) Don't use prompters. While the teacher and students may initially feel more comfortable with someone back stage to remind them of their lines, this can become a crutch and inhibits the learning of lines. A cooperative spirit can be fostered by encouraging actors to learn *all* lines, so that they can "whisper" assistance as it is needed.

Turning Stories Into Plays

Students have become sufficiently adept at utilizing a prepared script when they can memorize their lines, come in on cue, and create appropriate characterizations. With the background gained from using teacher-made scripts, they are then ready to actively participate in adapting plays from stories themselves. Many of the procedures described in the first phase are the same for adapting plays and need no further clarification. The following nine steps briefly outline the process used for this phase that encourages children to "bring stories to life":

1) Read a story aloud to children—with all the dramatic intensity you can muster. Fables and folk tales are especially useful for this purpose. One fifth-grade class did a lively rendition of the English folk tale "Molly Whuppie." Molly outwits a giant, then returns to steal a sword, a purse, and a ring. She then gaily escapes over the bridge of one hair.

2) Have several children relate sections of the story in sequence from memory. Encourage paraphrasing into words with which the children feel comfortable.

3) Write the parts of the play down, section by section, in the children's own words (language experience style). Encourage children to copy the story neatly from the board, thus providing each child with his or her own script.

4) Have small groups of children "block," or roughly act out, each part of the play, or "scene." While this is being done, discuss possible props, scenery, and costumes that might be used, as well as where students would logically stand to recite each line.

5) Let children try out for parts that they would like to play. While even at this "more experienced stage" a popular vote is still not a good idea, children may now be guided into making suggestions as to who might successfully play each character.

6) As a group, brainstorm about how each character would look, talk, walk, and feel. Roles of all levels of importance should be considered in this session, from narrator to those involved in crowd   scenes.

7) While the play is in the rehearsal stage, the music teacher can be informed of the theme of the upcoming performance, and could select a couple of songs that would enhance the script. The art teacher might be willing to use some class time to help the children make scenery, and the parents can become involved by assisting with costumes and/or props.

8) Help   children   to   design   invitations   inviting   parents, administrators, and other classes to the performances.

9) Put on a *superb* performance that children have been intensely involved in from start to finish. Watch your students become confident actors and actresses!

Creating Original Drama

In my own experience, the most memorable and mind-stretching skits were the ones that children wrote themselves, as group efforts. They had gone from reading and acting out the words of others to bringing their *own* words to life. In addition, an almost tangible feeling of pride and cooperation was fostered with this creative undertaking.

To ensure the success of this most ambitious phase of the drama program; it is helpful to: 1) begin with simple, one-act skits; 2) divide the class, depending upon its size, into three or four small groups; and 3) provide each group of students with a "plot," or structure, to build from. While the directive "Write a play about whatever you wish . . ."

would seem to offer a wide open field, most students seem to appreciate a stimulus idea that inspires them.

One such idea that works well with intermediate level students is:

"Pretend you are a community of little animals living happily together in the forest when one day you find you are about to be visited by a strange new visitor who wants to talk with all of you.

"What or who would the visitor be?

"What would the visitor want?

"What would the visitor have to say?

"How would the lives of the animals be changed?"

Such a stimulus provides the impetus for a brainstorming session by the group. One student acts as "recorder" and, as ideas are finalized within the group, the skit is crystallized onto paper. Generally, the children will consciously create the number of characters needed to cast every member of their group, and those who contribute ideas are cast into the roles that they themselves have created. The teacher, meanwhile, floats between groups, offering suggestions where needed and furnishing assistance in the spelling of words that students want to use.

The following play was written by a group of six fourth-grade students in response to the above stimulus idea. The six children cast themselves into the roles of narrator (who introduced the play and the characters), rabbit, bear, frog, squirrel, and the "Mysterious Something."

Cast:
Squirrel
Frog
Bear
Rabbit
Mysterious Something

Props:
Tree, sign pinned to tree, stump, several bushes.

Scene:
Animals are in the forest gathered around the sign on the tree.

The Mysterious Something

Squirrel: Hey, everybody! There's a sign hanging on that tree!
Frog: A sign? There has never been a sign on that tree before!
Bear: What does the sign say, Squirrel?

Squirrel: I don't know. I never learned how to read.

Frog: I can't read either.

Bear: Neither can I.

Rabbit: I can read! I can read!

Frog: Hooray for Rabbit! Tell us what the sign says, Rabbit.

Rabbit: Now, let me see. Oh dear, oh dear, *oh dear*, **OH DEAR!**

Bear: Is it bad news, Rabbit?

Frog: Is it a message from the king?

Squirrel: Is it something terrible?

Rabbit: I'm really not sure. It may be good . . .

All others: Yay!!

Rabbit: . . . or it may be bad!

Others: (groaning) Ohhhhh!

Rabbit: I'll read it out loud to you and then you can judge for yourselves—the sign says "To Whom It May Concern."

Squirrel: That means US!

Rabbit: Shhh! "To Whom It May Concern: On Wednesday morning when the sun is at its highest in the sky, I am coming to the forest to live. *If* the animals of the forest treat me well, I will be a good neighbor. *But,* if the animals of the forest make me angry, or hurt my feelings, or upset my temper, I will punish them with a *terrible* punishment! I shall expect all of the animals to be under this tree to greet me when I arrive. Yours truly, The Mysterious Something."

Squirrel (jumping up): I don't like it! Not one bit! Did you hear the part about a *terrible* punishment??! I bet this "mysterious something" is some kind of a giant!

Bear: He sounds more like a dragon to me—the kind that breathes fire (roar)!

Frog: Wait a minute, guys! Did you hear the part about being a good neighbor? Maybe the "mysterious something" is gentle and kind. *Maybe* he's a puppy dog! (others laugh)

Rabbit: We'll find out soon enough what the mysterious something is. The sign says he's coming Wednesday when the sun is at its highest in the sky.

Squirrel: And today is Wednesday!

Frog: And look! The sun is almost at the top of the sky!

Rabbit: Listen, everybody! I think I hear footsteps!

Squirrel: Oh, he's coming! He's *coming!* The "Mysterious Something" is coming!

Frog: If only we had some idea of what the mysterious something is. If *only* we had some clue. Then I wouldn't be so frightened!

Rabbit: I know! Maybe if one of us stood on that tree stump, he might get a glimpse of the Mysterious Something coming through the forest.

Frog: Good idea, Rabbit!

Rabbit: Bear, you're the tallest. Climb up on that stump and see what you can see.

Squirrel: Can you see anything, Bear?

Bear: Yes, yes! I see the Mysterious Something! She looks friendly! Here she comes now! (Bear points and all other animals look curiously.)

Animals: (bowing) Good afternoon, Mysterious Something.

MS: Good afternoon! I see you all read my sign.

Squirrel: Oh, yes, we did!

Frog: It is a very interesting sign!

Rabbit: Most interesting!

Bear: But. . .

MS: But what?

Bear: But it needs a little explaining!

MS: I thought it was perfectly clear. What would you like me to explain?

Bear: Well, you ask us not to make you angry. What kinds of things make you angry?

Squirrel: And you ask us not to upset your temper. What kinds of things upset your temper?

Rabbit: And you ask us not to hurt your feelings. What kinds of things hurt your feelings?

MS: Okay! I see what the problem is! Very well, I will explain. The thing that makes me angriest is GREED. The thing that most upsets my temper is DISHONESTY. And the thing that is most certain to hurt my feelings is an UNKIND WORD.

Bear: Well, we promise never to be greedy. We wouldn't want to make you angry!

Squirrel: And we promise we will never be dishonest! We wouldn't want to upset your temper!

Rabbit: And we promise never to say unkind words! We wouldn't want to hurt your feelings!

Frog: And most of all, we promise that we will be your good friends and neighbors.

MS: If we *all* follow those rules, I am sure we will get along just fine!

Animals: Welcome to our forest, Mysterious Something, welcome to our forest!

*****

Bringing reading to life as suggested in this three-phase drama program creates a definite aura of excitement and positive feeling toward learning. But teachers are often amazed when they stop to consider the breadth of reading skills and attitudes that can be developed and reinforced in the process:

1) Listening comprehension is heightened. At no other juncture in the reading program are children so intensely motivated to listen. With drama, they can readily see the purpose for attentive listening to each other.

2) Sequencing skills are polished. While recalling scenes for the purpose of blocking them, students naturally must pay careful attention to the order of events, as well as to the cause and effect of related happenings.

3) Vocabulary is increased. While adapting "Molly Whuppie," for example, children may choose to recite the giant's words verbatim: "If once again you cross my path, thy shall feel the giant's *wrath*!" By the end of the play, every child has integrated the word "wrath" into his or her meaning vocabulary.

4) High motivation to read other similar stories. After adapting Molly Whuppie, students will want to reread this and all other stories in the English Fable book from which it came.

5) Basic sight vocabulary is reinforced. The words that children use most often in their normal speaking will be incorporated into their scripts. To illustrate, "The Mysterious Something" contains nearly 75 percent of all the Dolch Basic Sight Words. The repeated readings required to memorize such scripts will greatly reinforce, as well as add many new words to, the students' sight vocabulary.

6) Oral language is developed. Fluent oral language is a prerequisite for reading proficiency, yet there is often not adequate provision for its expression in the classroom. Drama fulfills this need.

7) A positive self-concept is promoted. Children work together and become "somebody" through dramatic portrayals. Standing before an audience and provoking laughter (in comic roles) and earning applause (in *all* roles) fosters an emergent "I am capable" attitude.

Summary

There is probably no better avenue than drama to reach children on a truly affective level. Children thrive on a medium that allows them to create with their minds and bodies using expressive movement as well as words.

Aside from being a great natural motivator, drama improves a child's reading ability by providing listening practice, reinforcing sequencing skills, introducing new vocabulary, providing for the refinement of oral language skills, as well as reviewing basic sight vocabulary. It can also lead some children to eagerly read new stories similar to that from which the play was adapted.

Not least of all, used on a routine basis drama can be a way to systematically enhance the self-concepts of students in the reading program. One fifth-grade budding actor summed it up this way: "I really helped to write this play and put it on with my class. Not only did I write it, but I also sang a song and got to be the mayor and helped kids memorize their lines. I learned one important thing about myself—I know now I can do just about *anything* when I put my mind to it!"

References

Bolton, G. (1984). *Drama as Education*. London: Longman House.

Cecil, N.L. (1989). *Freedom Fighters: Affective Teaching of the Language Arts*. Salem, WI: Sheffield Publishing Co.

Corathers, D. (1991). "Theatre Education: Seeking Balance Between Stage and Classroom." *ASCD Update*, November.

Cowen, J., ed. (1983). *Teaching Reading Through the Arts*. Newark: International Reading Association.

De La Mare, W. (1946). *Tales Told Again*. Ill. by Alan Howard. New York: Knopf.

Dolch, E.W. (1936). "A Basic Sight Vocabulary." *Elementary School Journal* 36. February: 456-460.

Sanders, S. (1970). *Creating Plays with Children*. New York: Citation Press.

Way, B. (1967). *Development Through Drama*. London: Longman Group.

Chapter Eight
The Incredible Instructional Cloze

It appears that the cloze technique can be valuable when
it is used as a vehicle to promote discussion of
language—to reflect upon and make explicit what
students know about how language works . . .
—Patrick Finn, *Helping*
Children Learn to Read

One of the most exciting times of the day in one third grade
classroom is the very first activity of the morning, just after the students
have all come spilling in. With a hasty "Good Morning" they rush to
their seats to try to come up with the most original and creative words
to fill in the blanks of the puzzle-like paragraph on the blackboard.
After attendance is taken and various other morning rituals are taken
care of, the teacher goes up to the blackboard and begins what every
child has been waiting for—the participation part of the cloze exercise.
The teacher asks, "Who has a 'super good' word for the first blank?"
Every hand goes up and occasionally, with youthful bursts of
enthusiasm, someone shouts out an answer (this is, of course, "bad
manners," but the teacher is secretly pleased).

Cloze was once "misunderstood," but in the last few years the
procedure has gained increased popularity as a respectable teaching tool.
There is much current research to indicate that this recent acclaim is
well-deserved. An example is a study by Sampson, Valmont, and Allen
(1982) that explored just how effective the cloze could be as an
alternative to more traditional reading approaches. The study found the
cloze to be a significant success in improving the reading comprehension
and divergent production (the "fine tuning" of vocabulary) of a group of
second-grade students who had received 1) sufficient exposure to cloze
exercises, 2) ample teacher-guided discussions regarding the purpose and
method of using the procedure; and 3) considerable practice using cloze.
In the discussions accompanying the exercises in this study, synonyms

for the original response were not only accepted, but encouraged and highly praised. Pupils soon found that there are lots of ways, all essentially "correct," of saying the same thing. A deeper understanding and respect for the fine shades of meaning in the English language evolved.

As the above study reveals, cloze is an ideal way to improve a child's reading comprehension and broaden vocabulary. It is also incredibly easy for teachers to construct, while being fun for the children. Therefore, it is a perfect complement to an Affective Reading Program.

Cloze actually goes beyond the demands of an ordinary reading lesson by requiring the child to participate in a complex hierarchical procedure which involves 1) the decoding of words; 2) the understanding of those words; 3) the syntactic analysis of how those words fit together grammatically; and 4) comprehension of each sentence, as well as how each relates to the meaning of the whole paragraph.

Instead of isolating each of these skills into meaningless workbook drills as is so often done with basal programs, cloze allows the child to experiment with these skills naturally. It provides a place in the curriculum where children can be introduced to little interesting, incidental facts in a "game-like" context.

Example: He was in the _____ of a good book _____ he heard the clanging _____ a bell, which interrupted _____ serenity.

In the above example, consider for a minute the intricate procedure *you* had to follow in order to fill in the blanks. First, you had to decode all the words. If you didn't know the word "clanging," for instance, you had to "sound it out" or use the context to figure it out. Second, you had to either know or guess from context the meanings of all the words used. Third, you had to call upon your knowledge of English grammar to reach the conclusion that a preposition, specifically the preposition "of," was needed after the word "clanging." Finally, in order to fill in any of the blanks you had to have an understanding of the underlying "sense" of the sentence. Many "mental gymnastics" were performed without your even thinking about them!

To devise a cloze exercise, one can select reading matter from any material on or below the children's reading level: favorite trade books, text books, children's encyclopedias, magazines—anything of general interest to your class will do. Then:

1) Choose 250 words at random from the text;

2) Don't make any deletions from the first or last sentences, to allow readers to grasp the "sense" of the paragraph;

3) Delete every "*n*th" word. The more deletions, the harder the cloze exercise, so you might want to start by taking out every tenth word;

4) Leave a line of uniform size where each word was.

The success of the cloze, as the previously mentioned study indicates, as well as teachers who use it will testify, depends on careful introduction of the procedure to the children and plenty of daily, guided practice. Fifteen or twenty minutes expended on the cloze every day, combined with the other features of an Affective Reading Program, are recommended. It is suggested also that certain standard steps are followed (Bortnick and Lopardo, 1973; Cecil, 1983):

1) Introduce the cloze as a kind of a challenge, where there are no right or wrong answers but where the student is expected to think up "interesting and appropriate words."

2) Have children copy the cloze exercise exactly as it is written on the blackboard or overhead transparency.

3) Instruct the students to read the *entire* passage before they fill in any blanks. They must do this in order to get the whole meaning of the paragraph.

4) After they have read the whole paragraph, tell students to reread the paragraph, this time filling in all the blanks as they go along, with suitable words. No time limit should be set (for this reason, teachers may opt to use cloze before opening exercises, so that each child can set his or her own pace). Teachers should tell students any words which they are not able to decode.

5) When they are finished, ask students to volunteer to give their answers for each blank. The teacher (or student) fills them in on the blackboard or transparency.

6) Certain "rich" synonyms are pointed out and praised effusively as being more descriptive than the original text:

Example: Original text: It was a *hot* night.
        Student version: It was a *sweltering* night.

The high motivational appeal lies in the way the teacher deliberately "plays up" the superiority of certain words the students have chosen over the more staid, controlled vocabulary of the original text. Obviously, every student will not always come up with a "better" synonym, but teachers are always amazed to find that, at one time or another, each child in the class manages to think of a few responses that surpass the originals (this is, of course, in the teacher's subjective judgment, but does it matter?). The praise and positive feedback children receive for these contributions make cloze a challenging activity that they thoroughly enjoy.

7) Explain (gently) why certain responses are *not* suitable if they change the grammar or meaning of a sentence or paragraph:

Example: Original text: The *fat* lady waddled down the street.

Student's version: The *lively* lady waddled down the street.

Clearly, much can be understood about reading for meaning as the teacher explains why "lively" would not be a wise choice in the above sentence, because the word "waddle" suggests a slow-moving, portly woman rather than a "lively" one.

8) Finally, compare the completed version of the whole paragraph done by the class with the original text. Discuss as a group how the passage has been improved by the creative additions of class members.

9) Students can be encouraged to keep track of their own scores, attempting each time to get a higher number of suitable words in the blanks. Generally speaking, about half of the words correct would indicate that the material is on the student's instructional reading level.

Using these procedures, the cloze can offer a variety of vocabulary enhancers with individual handouts, or as a whole class activity on the overhead projector. Here are a few examples of uses for cloze for vocabulary instruction:

• Provide two passages of text for children with the same words deleted in each. Ask children to create entirely different moods in each of the passages by varying their choice of words, e.g., "It was a
cold   dreary
bright and *sunny* day."

• Have children devise their own cloze passages using chapter summaries, tradebooks, or newspaper articles. Invite children to trade their cloze activities with each other.

• For more advanced learners, provide a series of selected words to be incorporated into a text. Instruct them to write a passage, leaving a blank for each of the words provided (Klein, Peterson & Simington, 1991).

By following the listed procedures, much success has been noted by enthusiastic proponents of cloze, but two major concerns have frequently been voiced.

The first concern relates to the "impulsive child" of whom there appear to be at least a few in every elementary classroom. This type of child seems reluctant to complete the first step in the execution of the cloze; that is he or she tends not to read all the way through the cloze passage first before filling in the deletions, thereby missing much important information that can often be culled from an initial overview of the paragraph. This situation can often be rectified with a preintroduction to the cloze called the "musical cloze" (Cecil, 1984). Any selection of music with which the students are thoroughly familiar can be used for this purpose. A favorite Christmas carol, for example, or perhaps the latest Top Forty hit would be tape-recorded with every third note deleted (this time leaving no lines intact) to produce a "quasi-cloze" format. Simply by playing the first several unconnected notes alone, children prone to rash guessing will begin to get the idea that they must hear the whole thing first; the blank notes are dependent upon additional information to be gleaned by listening to the entire recording. Next, when the whole passage is played, students can then employ the technique of "cloze" to complete the musical composition. While this musical cloze is clearly not as demanding as a regular cloze reading exercise, the rough analogy can be useful. This activity may be the "little extra" that is needed to stress the importance of thoroughly reading a cloze passage before filling in the blank spaces.

A second concern with cloze as part of a reading program has been a lingering worry expressed by some teachers that cloze has a tendency to frustrate students who are used to perfect papers. Others become devastated by what they erroneously perceive as "failure." These observations can be readily appreciated when one recalls that a child need only get approximately half of the responses correct to achieve what the teacher will consider a "good score," or one that would suggest that the material is on the child's instructional level. Obviously, with students conditioned to a more traditional system where achieving 90 percent or better is the ultimate goal, receiving a score of only half, or 50 percent, on a cloze would not engender the same feelings of success.

To counteract this concern with the significance of scores, one solution is comparing cloze scores with baseball scores. Most children readily understand that in the game of baseball, getting a hit three out of ten times—or "batting .300"—is considered doing quite well. An analogy can be made pointing out to children that in cloze exercises, as in baseball, one does not expect to have 100 percent success to be considered "good at it." The analogy can be stretched further to compare a certain wonderfully descriptive word ("sweltering" as opposed to "hot") with a home run, which is the batter's only hit in that game. In both situations, quality is more important than quantity.

Finally, the discussion phase of the cloze procedure cannot be emphasized strongly enough! Students consistently praised and reinforced for the refreshing words that they offer as synonyms for the original can learn to view this type of "reward" as a viable trade-off for the more common reinforcement of a high score.

Summary

Used on a daily basis, the cloze procedure can be an exciting component of an Affective Reading Program and one which the whole class can participate in and enjoy. Every student can, at some time, come up with new and different words that will serve to upgrade the original cloze passage. Having these contributions accepted can foster positive feelings in students toward words, and how they can be used in the reading and writing processes. Care must be taken to ensure that children come to see cloze as a non-threatening reading lesson with a "game-like" challenge, in some ways similar to their favorite computer game. Students can be guided toward regarding cloze not as a "test" with all of its negative connotations, but rather as an open-ended personal "contest" in which the student's aim is to continually better his or her own performance with constant practice.

References

Bortnick, R., and G. Lopardo. (1973). "An Instructional Application of the Cloze Procedure," *Journal of Reading* 16. January: 296-300.

Cecil, N.L. (1985). "Instructional Cloze: Confronting Some Common Concerns," *Reading Horizons* 25, no. 2: 95-97.

Finn, P.J. (1985). *Helping Children Learn to Read*. New York: Random House.

Klein, M.L., S. Peterson, and L. Simington. (1991). *Teaching Reading in the Elementary Grades*. Boston: Allyn and Bacon.

Sampson, M.R., W.J. Valmont and R.V. Allen. (1982). "The Effects of Instructional Cloze on the Comprehension, Vocabulary, and Divergent Production of Third-Grade Students," *Reading Research Quarterly* 16, no. 3: 389-399.

Chapter Nine

Reading Aloud to Children

A word is dead
When it is said,
Some say.

I say it just
Begins to live
That day.
—Emily Dickinson

Some children, if they are lucky, spend countless hours of their early childhood years safely nestled in the lap of a parent or relative, listening to their favorite stories or nursery rhymes being read aloud. Perhaps if these tiny persons could verbally communicate their innermost feelings at such times, they might confide that, yes, they enjoy the stories, but they especially cherish the warm "snuggling" that this sharing time provides.

Reading to children in school fosters similar warm feelings. Favorable educational outcomes are also noted: Children who are consistently read to perform significantly better in reading comprehension and vocabulary than those who do not receive this exposure (Carbo, 1978).

Studies in home settings have shown that vocabulary growth, increased awareness of the nature of written language, growth in background knowledge, eagerness to read, learning to read before school, and even success in beginning reading, are all associated with storybook reading (Teale, 1984). A study by Feitelson, Kita and Goldstein (1986) provides an even more powerful argument for reading aloud to children: their study showed that regular reading aloud to children was positively correlated with greater listening comprehension, more active use of language, and increased ability to decode new words, building an excellent foundation for continued literacy growth.

Reading a variety of literature to children develops background experience vicariously for those children limited in that area, and engenders an understanding of the "special language" of books (Roney, 1984).

Wiseman (1992) offers several additional reasons why teachers should read aloud to children:

• Reading aloud provides a good, nonthreatening role model of standard English language—especially critical for children for whom English is a second language.

• Children will happily listen to stories which may be too difficult for them to read themselves; thus, they "broaden their horizons."

• Reading aloud to children can help them to encounter interesting characters and events that may motivate them to read more. A child's first introduction to *Amelia Bedelia* and her zany antics, for example, may encourage children to look for sequels.

• Reading aloud provides exposure to a wide variety of literary genres. The nine-year-old who is "stuck" in a horse story "rut" may realize that there are other books that are of interest to her.

Teachers of primary-age children know that reading aloud to students is important; therefore, a story time is usually built into the curriculum for the early grades. Somewhere around the fourth grade, however, children are expected to have reached a measure of independence in decoding. After that time, reading aloud to children often ceases and children are then expected to just "read to themselves."

Teachers at *all* grade levels (yes, even high school teachers!) who wish to implement an Affective Reading Program must continue to read to their students—and often. While twenty minutes was the recommended allotment for the Read Aloud component of this program, this figure should be considered only the BAREST MINIMUM. Several other times in the day children should have an opportunity to hear material of varying formats and lengths, such as magazine articles, quotations, poems, special passages, song lyrics, newspaper items, etc., as well as more prosaic "story books." *Any* leftover time during the day can be spent reading to children, such as the few minutes remaining before lunch, after gym class, or between academic subjects. These additional reading sessions might vary from a few seconds to many minutes. In an Affective Reading Program one might often hear a teacher say, "Okay . . . we have a couple of minutes. Let's hurry back to Charlotte and see how she's getting along at the fair." This activity is not only practical in terms of "good stewardship" of time, but it aptly models the behavior of the avid reader who quickly gets back to the novel he or she is reading—at any and every possible moment.

What Material to Choose

Reading aloud is the best purpose for which to bring the entire class together to share an enjoyable reading experience without competition or anxiety. Almost anything can be read to children during Read Aloud time. At other times in the program, children are urged to use the "Rule of Thumb" in order to know when to discard books with too many unfamiliar words; the same is NOT true during the Read Aloud time. Traditional age, grade, or independent levels are of little importance here. Instead, through actively listening, children can be stretched and prodded in many different directions. These are the moments when children can be comfortably challenged and broadened in their literary tastes, while the frustration caused by lack of rapid decoding skills is singularly avoided. Children quickly learn to get the sense of new vocabulary through contextual clues, and they begin to extract new ideas and concepts commensurate with their own maturity and experience. For example, Hemingway's *The Old Man and the Sea* can be listened to and enjoyed by fifth-graders, yet tenth-graders will appreciate it at a deeper level.

Books may be chosen, sometimes, simply because they hold special appeal to the teacher. Traditional favorites from the teacher's childhood, as well as new-found friends that the teacher is currently excited about, are ideal. It would be most appropriate with these special favorites to preface the reading with a personal account of the book's meaning to the teacher, or special memories that are brought to mind by it. For example, one teacher always begins the reading of Wilder's *Little House on the Prairie* series by telling the class how she "devoured" all eight books in the series during a wonderful week off from school due to a severe blizzard. The teacher's personal feel for the book can generate a contagious enthusiasm that demonstrates to children that reading really is a most enjoyable activity.

Another suggestion for material to read aloud may come from people, concepts, and events the class is studying in the content areas. For example, a unit on the Revolutionary War might be a good time to present an historical novel such as *Johnny Tremain*, while a bit of well-crafted nonfiction from the *National Geographic* magazine could help bring to life a science lesson about reptiles. School librarians are usually able to recommend a variety of interesting trade books that can help to reinforce anything from a science lesson on animals (Bonner's *A Penguin Year*) to concepts in math (Anno's *Counting House*). The reading aloud of trade books in these diverse areas has the additional advantage of presenting concepts in a manner than enhances the children's regular text book, yet allows children for whom the text is too difficult to participate in learning.

At other times, books and other reading material might be chosen to help individual children, or the class as a whole, to work out certain problems that are currently facing them. For example, the topics of death, divorce, child abuse, physical and mental handicaps, and suicide, to name only a few, are ones that are relevant to children in today's world. Set in palatable story formats by such talented authors as Judy Blume, Richard Peck, or Norma Kline, these books often provoke discussions that are important in promoting emotional growth and a sense of well-being. While not all problems can hope to be "solved" in such a manner, often children gain new insights into how others might handle the concerns that are facing them through these vicarious experiences. They also begin to acquire an appreciation for reading as an activity that can help them to better understand themselves and their world. *The Bookfinder* is an annotated bibliography of over a thousand children's books, categorized into every conceivable socially relevant topic, that would be helpful to a teacher interested in bringing such issues to the classroom.

Finally, many current lists of new children's books that have gained literary acclaim are available from school librarians. The Caldecott winners, for example, have been recognized for outstanding illustrations, while the books receiving Newbery Awards are considered exceptionally well written literature for children. These books are excellent choices for ensuring that students are exposed to the highest quality of recently written children's books. Also, each year the International Reading Association puts out a list of the most outstanding new books, as selected by children—"The Children's Choices." These books are often "best bets," as they have been proven to have tremendous appeal, not only to the more sophisticated tastes of adults, but to a large sample of randomly selected children.

How to Read Aloud to Children

While most teachers (hopefully) are avid readers themselves, not all have had much experience or practice in reading aloud; especially those who teach the intermediate grades and higher. Others who *do* spend considerable time reading aloud might also benefit from the following suggestions.

First and foremost, it is important to feel comfortable with the material that is read. While it is probably not necessary (or practical) to practice reading *everything* that is to be read before a group of children, some general reading "rehearsals" should be made before the Read

Aloud program is implemented. The teacher, for example, might want to practice reading a story to a spouse, friend, another teacher, or to him or herself in front of a mirror. Careful attention should be given to the pitch, vocal quality, and modulation of the voice. We have *all* heard speakers who have threatened to put us to sleep! As teachers of young people, we must be especially aware of the need to exude enthusiasm.

Poems, particularly, should be read aloud several times in order for teachers to feel at ease with their special kinds of cadence. In this manner, children can be shown that poetry is written to convey a personal message and/or feeling, and is not always a "sing-songy" nursery rhyme.

Also, the pronunciation of unfamiliar words should be checked. Often adults are able to read and understand many words that they are not always able to pronounce correctly. As an example, I will always remember a conversation in which I mentioned that an idea was totally "Anna Thema" (anáthema) to me, and was later quietly corrected—and thoroughly embarrassed!

When reading aloud, some teachers with a "theatrical bent," and for whom lack of reading practice is not a problem, go to the opposite extreme. They tend to make a story read aloud into a major production. As was stated, enthusiasm is extremely important and some characterization can help to bring the story to life. However, too much drama can draw attention away from the material and instead focus it on "the performance."

The story itself—and not the presenter—should always be the center of attention. Likewise, distracting mannerisms, such as clearing one's throat, head scratching, etc., should be avoided. In a similar vein, pacing back and forth while reading can prevent children from concentrating on what they are hearing. The teacher, instead, might want to perch unobtrusively, yet comfortably, on a desk top or chair and remain as still as possible for the duration of the Read Aloud session.

Another distraction can be the illustrations in picture story books. While often beautifully drawn additions to the text, they can most effectively be used as "teasers." A few pictures should be shown, but with discretion, whetting the students' appetites to see the rest of the pictures (and, of course, reread the entire book). Another reason for not stopping to show every illustration is that the continuity and the rhythm of the story are lost with such frequent interruptions. Additionally, reading aloud to children is the perfect time for encouraging listening skills and fostering creative imagining. Therefore, it seems logical that children should be allowed just to "listen carefully." They can then put their *own* faces to the characters they are encountering, and picture their *own* special places created by the fantasies of their own minds. In this age of ultra-realistic video games and dolls almost as lifelike as humans, it seems listening to stories would be a good way to prevent imagining from becoming a "lost art."

Other Read Aloud Suggestions

When a picture story book—or any other material read to the class—has been completed, the next step is crucial: it should then be made readily available for children to pick up and reread on their own. If possible, multiple copies should be obtained. The desire to languish more casually on a recent literary experience, or to compare the author's illustrations with those of the child's fantasies will be very intense. Besides the literature that has just been read aloud, related material or other works by the same author can be "advertised" and placed strategically around the room for children to enjoy.

Finally, children should have an opportunity to listen to the reading of a wide variety of individuals. The differences in presentation and style are as varied as human beings themselves and thus add an important breadth to the listening experiences for children. These "guest readers" serve another, even more important function: Children *expect* that their teacher, and perhaps the librarian or principal, are "hooked" on this reading idea but they are most pleased to find that others, whom they don't relate to "education," also enjoy reading. School personnel, such as janitors, secretaries, and lunch room staff, are often delighted to be asked to come in and share a story with a class. A physical education instructor reading to the class can help establish a notion that people who are "into sports" can also be "into books." Community members, such as police officers and fire fighters, are often called upon as resources to talk to students about their careers. But these same persons, by spending just a few minutes reading to children, can also change certain stereotypes about "who is likely to enjoy reading."

Summary

The practice of consistently reading aloud to children not only makes them better readers but it introduces them to the wide variety of literature available for them to explore. It broadens and reaffirms the importance of their own experiences and helps children to understand themselves and their world. What they hear can open children to new ideas, events, and images that can help to enrich their lives.

Additionally, reading aloud to children in the school setting is likely to evoke memories of the special "snuggling" times of listening to stories with parents, or it may, for those who haven't been read to, present these warm feelings for the very first time. These special feelings are fundamental to an Affective Reading Program. In my elementary school teaching years, I would often begin reading a story and, when my eyes left the page, be amused to find little chairs inching forward to where I had perched, until I had many small elbows in my lap and several heads resting softly against my arms. The "offenders" would often try to disguise the purpose of their movements by crowing, "But I can't HEAR from back there!" but I wasn't fooled. Reading aloud to children just naturally encourages this bond of feelings between teacher and child and, just as importantly, creates warm and comfortable associations with reading.

References

American Guidance Service. (1977). *The Bookfinder*.

Anno, M. (1982). *The Counting House*. New York: Philomel Books.

Bonner, S. (1981). *A Penguin Year*. New York: Delacorte Press.

Carbo, M. (1978). "Teaching Reading with Talking Books," *The Reading Teacher* 32, no. 3, December: 267-273.

Feitelson, D., B. Kita, and Z. Goldstein. (1986). "Effects of Listening to Series Stories on First Graders' Comprehension and Use of Language." *Research in the Teaching of English*, 20, 339-356.

Roney, R.C. (1984). "Background Experience Is the Foundation of Success in Learning to Read," *The Reading Teacher* 38, no. 2, November: 196-199.

Teale, W.H. (1984). "Reading to Young Children: It's Significance for Literacy Development." In H. Goelman, A. Oberg and F. Smith (eds.) *Awakening to Literacy*, pp. 110-121. Exeter, NH: Heinemann.

Trelease, J. (1982). *The Read Aloud Handbook*. New York: Penguin Books.

Wiseman, D.L. (1992). *Learning to Read with Literature*. Boston: Allyn and Bacon.

Chapter Ten

The Total Teaching Triangle: Engaging the Parent

> The school should make clear that it regards the
> education of children as a team project in which the
> home and the school have a common interest.
> —Dallman, Rouch, Char, and Deboer,
> *The Teaching of Reading*

All teachers seem to report the same phenomenon. They are asked one question by parents far more often than any other: How can I help my child to become a better reader? The teacher is gratified by this willingness on the part of so many parents to do whatever they can to assist. But the teacher soon comes to realize that parents, without specific guidance, can easily fall into one of two categories: 1) those who are so anxious to help their child to succeed that they inadvertently transfer that anxiety to their child; and 2) parents—equally well-meaning—who would really love to help, but believe it is beyond their capabilities to do any "serious teaching."

Parents seek and deserve guidance so that they can naturally "spill" the child's reading program into the home. Children, on the other hand, are more open to learning when they perceive a real harmony in the relationship between their two worlds—their home life and their school life. Nothing, then, could contribute more to a child's positive feeling about reading than to have the teacher AND all those at home who are significant in the child's life involved in and caring about the reading program.

This chapter will describe some structural ways to develop communication between the home and school. It also outlines specific strategies that teachers can use to show parents how to work directly with their child, in an instructional capacity, at home. Finally, it will provide a host of suggestions that might be offered to parents who don't feel comfortable doing direct teaching, but who are still interested in exploring ways to contribute varied reading experiences for their child.

The Initial Connection

Good communication between the home and the school is crucial for a parent's understanding and support of the Affective Reading Program. Because this is true with most programs, some schools provide several parent-teacher conference days when teachers are free to talk with the parents about their child's progress. While this can be an ideal time to talk about the child's reading, several factors often interfere with a successful meeting taking place. First of all, many parents work during the day and cannot afford to take the time off to attend these sessions. Since it is not up to the teacher to judge the parents' priorities or work responsibilities, he or she must accept these concerns sympathetically and try, instead, to rectify the problem. Moving the time of the conference to later in the day—for example from 2 to 8:00 p.m. (with the teachers given the morning off)—is a possible solution. Such a plan has been successful in reaching parents who had previously been unable to attend conferences due to job conflicts (Loving and Estes, 1984).

Other parents may be reluctant to attend any school functions because they feel uncomfortable in the school environment. They themselves may not have done well in school and for them "The School" holds unpleasant memories—much as the dentist's office does to those who suffered many extractions as a child. As these parents are often the ones teachers *most* want to see in regard to a child's reading attitudes, one suggestion is that the teacher initially goes to them. A call or brief note saying the teacher will be in the area on such and such a day and could (s)he stop by to chat is rarely refused. Nothing "academic" needs to be discussed at this time. But a warm and accepting tone by the teacher often leads to the initial rapport which makes the parent's attendance at the next conference more likely.

In a similar vein, a third stumbling block is what I call "educational jargonese." Perhaps in an effort to make the field of education seem more truly a profession, we educators have acquired a large vocabulary of very specific educational terminology. "Dyslexia" is one such term (which no one, to my knowledge, has yet adequately defined!) that might be better described to parents more simply as "a problem with the child's reading." Many other such terms can be discussed in "laymen's talk" also, with the result that the parents feel they are capable of understanding what the teacher is talking about. Too many parents refrain from attending meetings concerning their child's progress

because they are convinced they are not bright enough to comprehend the teacher's "educated" language.

Parent-Teacher Conferencing

The parent-teacher conference can be a fruitful time for the teacher to explain, in clear terms, the child's reading program and the child's progress within that program. Moreover, it is the ideal time to let the parents know how much their partnership is needed to reinforce the notion upon which the Affective Reading Program is based: that reading is important and also very enjoyable. Before "lecturing" them on how to help their child at home, though, the parents often need some basic reassurance from you; they are concerned, and you need to let them know that their concern is justified. The following points are important to ponder in this regard:

1) Parents have a right to their anxiety. Wouldn't one expect a caring parent to be wondering how well Johnny is keeping up with his peers?

2) Similarly, "don't worry" is a phrase that has little value. Sympathize with the parents' concerns and then help them to be better informed. Share your evaluation of the child's reading strengths as well as weaknesses.

3) In general, be extremely sensitive to the feelings of the parents. Listen to them! Instead of blaming them for fostering negative attitudes, praise them for the concern they are demonstrating. Then, discuss the positive ways that they can join you in improving the child's reading.

Direct Parent Involvement in Reading

Some parents are willing and able to work with the child at home to encourage reading progress. You might want to assure parents that assisting their child in this way does not take a "deep" understanding of phonics and/or instructional techniques, as some parents fear. It simply requires common sense and a good deal of patience. If the teacher and the parents feel this is the case, a few suggestions should be given as guidelines. These might be provided to the parents in written format and then carefully discussed so that any questions or concerns could be addressed:

1) Set aside fifteen minutes a day to have your child read to you. Make sure that the allotted time in *no way* interferes with the child's favorite activities.

2) Have children bring home books that interest them from school to read, or help them select books from the public library. The only

stipulation is that the book must *never* be too hard for the child! If the child is unfamiliar with more than five words on a page, gently direct him or her to an easier book on the same subject.

3) Make the reading time a "treat"—not a "treatment." If the sessions are *not* pleasant for the child you're doing more harm than good.

4) Since reading out loud requires more skills than silent reading, let the child first read the passage to him or herself. This "rehearsal" will build confidence and give the child a chance to show you some success.

5) If the child comes across an unfamiliar word, say nothing, but silently count to three. If the child has then successfully figured out the word, offer praise. If not, gently "feed" the child the word and let him/her continue.

6) Write down unfamiliar words for the child to review.

7) At the end of the child's reading of the passage, ask him or her what the passage was about.

8) Ask a couple of questions about the story that have more than one answer to encourage thinking. "Why?" and "What if . . ." questions are always good.

9) Find something to praise in the gaining confidence, smooth reading expression, or being able to talk about what was read. *Don't* be discouraged if the child does not read as well as you expect; like anything else, it takes practice.

10) Try to really enjoy listening to the child's reading. At first this may be difficult, but when you can both *relax* and *pleasantly share the experience*, you will begin to note improvement in the child's reading. Then it really will become more and *more* enjoyable!

Indirect Parent Involvement

Some parents are vitally interested in their child's reading, but feel they lack the time, the talent, or the temperament to read with them. It's best to trust their judgment in this matter. However, these parents need to be assured that much can still be done in the home to create positive attitudes toward reading without actually working with the child directly. Some suggestions for a more indirect approach to developing a child's reading are the following:

1) Take your child to the library as often as possible, preferably once a week.

2) Subscribe to a children's magazine that interests your child. Also, give books as presents. The teacher or librarian can provide some suggestions of suitable possibilities.

3) Let your child read recipes to you, and on occasion perhaps help him or her to cook something by following the directions.

4) When traveling, ask your child to read the signs for you.

5) When buying board games or computer disks for your child, select those that require extensive reading of directions.

6) Encourage your children to read to each other.

7) Let your child write up the shopping list as you call out the items; have the items read back to you.

8) Find a "pen-pal" for your child so that (s)he will be encouraged to write letters and read those that are received.

9) Read to your child as often as you can.

10) Choose a theme and ask all family members to write about the theme. Share the writing at meals or other family gatherings. If you have a camcorder, encourage children to write about family outings or celebrations, language experience style (Snyder, 1991) to provide "text" for the "movie."

11) Have a specific silent reading time for your family, much like sustained silent reading (SSR), where all family members stop all other activity and read for ten or fifteen minutes.

12) Finally, show your child that you value reading as a worthwhile activity. Frequently mention what you are reading. Above all, let the child *see* you reading.

Aside from actual planned conferences to relay information and suggestions, there are several other approaches that can be used to communicate with parents about a child's reading.

Readiness Booklet

Perhaps the best time to reach parents and invite them to join in the "teaching triangle" is at the beginning of their child's academic career. Several teachers might volunteer to speak with parents informally as they bring their children in to be registered for kindergarten. This initial phase might be the ultimate time to help them realize their important place in the reading progress of their children. At this time suggestions could be offered for direct and indirect parent involvement, as mentioned previously. Additionally, inexpensive literature can be given out to the parent, outlining the way to provide language experiences, develop reading readiness skills, and to offer specific tips on how and what to read to their children. One such item that would fill the bill is an easy to read pamphlet entitled "Helping Children to Learn about Reading," which can be obtained in large quantities at minimal cost from:

National Association for
the Education of Young Children
1834 Connecticut Avenue N.W.
Washington, D.C. 20009

Another document, which addresses the role of parents in greater depth, is an easy to read purse-size booklet called *Encourage Your Child to Read* (Larrick, 1980). Though a bit more costly, it gives many specific suggestions to parents.

Parents Newsletter

Parents face criticism from the news media about the nation's schools almost daily. They are often bewildered by the battle cry of "We have to return to the basics!" because they are not really sure if "the basics" are being taught in their child's school. An attractive, simply-written newsletter sent to parents several times a year can explain how "the basics" are taught and continuously reinforced in the Affective Reading Program. It can also be a vehicle through which to convey some of the suggestions for parents previously discussed. Additionally, any recurring questions that parents have been asking can be addressed in the newsletter.

Progress Notes

Another way to keep parents well informed is to send, at frequent intervals, a "progress note" home with a book that the child has just successfully finished reading. The note, written in a positive, "congratulatory" tone, might include a couple of open-ended questions for the parent to ask the child, as well as several vocabulary words to review. Then the parent might be asked to listen to the child read a passage that he or she particularly liked so that the parent can share in this happy experience of completing a book and, above all, help celebrate the success that the child has enjoyed.

Family Reading Day

A special idea to bring parents to school for an occasion other than the traditional parent-teacher conferences is the Family Reading Day. Any number of activities can be planned that have to do with parents and children sharing reading. For example, parents might be asked ahead of time to bring in their favorite children's book to share with the class, if they wish. Choral reading can be done with parents and

children taking appropriate (or inappropriate!) roles. Art activities can also be planned, such as making and playing reading games, or constructing dioramas or murals in connection with a book that the child has just read.

The Family Reading Day, which might be scheduled several times a year, also works well in collaboration with a Book Fair or Book Swap. A Book Fair can be organized with the assistance of a local book store or a children's book publisher, such as Scholastic. A Book Swap, on the other hand, requires less advanced planning, and can be arranged simply by having children bring in old books from home. The teacher can help by explaining to the parents how to match books to readers.

Summary

To suggest that the relationship between the child, the home, and the school is a "triangle affair" is certainly nothing new. But it is not always appreciated that such a tremendous amount of communication is required to make this affair work—as in any relationship. Teachers often need to be the "prime movers" in order to get the relationship off the ground. Much time spent on the preparation of specific "how to" materials is required. Modification of customary schedules and compromise for the parents' benefit is often called for. Even visiting reluctant parents at home may be necessary so that they begin to feel at ease and know they are 'valued" rather than "evaluated." Whatever the cost in time and effort, a united front between parent(s) and teacher is the ultimate way to let children know that reading is a positive and worthwhile activity at home, as well as at school. The following poem poignantly expresses the need for this triangular bond:

Unity

I dreamt I stood in a studio
And watched two sculptors there.
The clay they used was a young child's mind
And they fashioned it with care.
One was a teacher—the tools he used
Were books, music, and art.
The other, a parent, worked with a guiding hand,
And a gentle loving heart.
Day after day, the teacher toiled
With touch that was deft and sure
While the parent labored by his side
And polished and smoothed it o'er.

> And each agreed they would have failed
> If each had worked alone.
> For behind the teacher stood the school
> And behind the parent, the home.
> —Author Unknown

Not even the most dynamic "master teacher" can do it alone.

References

Childrey, J.A., Jr. (1981). "Home Remedies for Reluctant Readers," from *Motivating Reluctant Readers*, ed. by A.J. Ciani. Newark, Delaware: International Reading Association.

Clinard, L. (1981). *The Reading Triangle*. Farmington Hills: Focus Publishing Co.

Dallman, M., R.L. Rouch, L.Y. Char, and J.L. DeBoer. (1982). *The Teaching of Reading*. New York: Holt, Rinehart and Winston.

Larrick, N. (1980). *Encourage Your Child to Read: A Parent's Primer*. New York: Dell Publishing Co., Inc.

Loving, J., and C. Estes. (1984). "Parents: Tapping a Productive Resource." Paper presented at Twelfth Plains Regional Conference of the International Reading Association, St. Louis, November.

Schickedanz, J.A. (1983). "Helping Children Learn about Reading." Washington: National Association for the Education of Young Children.

Snyder, G. (1991). "Parents, Teachers, Children, and Whole Language." In V. Froese (ed.) *Whole-Language: Practice and Theory*. Boston: Allyn and Bacon.

Chapter Eleven
Creating Classroom Authors

There is no art to writing but having something to say.
—Robert Frost

Curiously, the teacher glances over to the Writing Center, from which the sounds of hungry lions and tigers are echoing forth. Oh—Randy is just writing again. The little boy gazes intently at his paper, and is soon inspired by his drawing of the beasts as well as the fierce roars he is making them produce. He quickly finishes his story. Randy writes two or three stories a day in this manner and no one has ever told him to; he and the other students in the class simply enjoy putting their whimsical fantasies into written form.

Reading and writing and thinking are all pieces of the same puzzle and need not be separated. Because this is true reading, writing, and thinking skills naturally blend and flow throughout an Affective Reading Program. Words are understood to be the "sounds of thoughts" and the children are encouraged to bring their own special feelings and experiences to the writing process. The sensitive teacher knows that the child alone can best evaluate the intensity of experiences upon which he or she must draw for ideas. Therefore, the affective teacher studiously avoids rigid assignments of writing topics chosen at random from the repertoire of an adult mind. Rather, it is felt that the children must do their own selecting, developing, and deciding what will or will not be shared with others. After all, the motivation, the personality, and the experiences lie deep within the children themselves.

Most of us remember all too vividly the ordeal of "composition time." No matter how zealous we may have been at filling in our private little diaries, we approached the task of writing at school with distaste. It just seemed that the prim, anemic accounts produced for assignments were a far cry from the exciting adventures we conjured for ourselves when our creative powers were allowed to roam free. At school we wrote what we thought the teacher wanted to hear; at home we simply enjoyed using our fertile imaginations. Those childish stories written for personal pleasure, or for the delectation of the child's playmates, were usually crude and often illegible, but they invariably had *life*. In an Affective Reading Program a Writing Center is available at many times during the day for the children. There they are free to write down their most pressing thoughts and ideas whenever they feel so inspired, without the pressure of a contrived assignment, or fear of reproval for spelling mistakes or grammatic imperfections.

Setting Up a Writing Center

In the writing corner of an Affective Reading Program each child may begin, from the very first years of school, to write his or her own record, book, or other creation. Some of the child's writing will be for other children to read, just as he or she will read theirs. Children best understand the language of their classmates and with much voluntary experience with writing, they begin to use the language as freshly and creatively as only children can. Writing in this center is a continuous, on-going enterprise which increasingly captivates the children more and more as their skills and imagining prowess are called into play. Like anything else, the more the children practice, the more skilled they become; the more skilled they become, the more self-motivated they are to write.

From the initial stages, children can be encouraged to use pictures to help them communicate what they wish to say. Illustrating is usually a great treat for children and, especially with younger children, a story idea is often spontaneously generated by the inspiration of their own artistry.

Although in most classrooms illustrations are limited to the medium of crayon or pencil, young children are fascinated and inspired by such media as crayon batik, crayon etching, poster paints, or pasted paper cutouts. Older children can be tempted to experiment with charcoal, water color, acrylics, pastels, ink, or a combination of these. Simple instructions for the use of each technique, along with a sample of a typical end product are also useful in the center so that children can expand their expressive capabilities. Samples can be students' work obtained from the art teacher or the work of former students of the classroom teacher.

The Writing Center benefits from media appropriate to the age of the students, as well as paint brushes, colored markers, rulers, erasers, scissors, pastes, large construction paper for covers, and either clear contact paper, acetate, or laminating equipment to protect finished products. At least two work spaces should be designated in the center;

one for the actual writing, and the other for illustrating books chosen for publication and making book covers. A typewriter (or several, if possible) is also useful, as well as a tape recorder with a headset. Music without lyrics, such as "Hall of the Mountain King" or "The William Tell Overture" is often an additional source of inspiration for young writers.

Paper is also an important issue in a Writing Center. Though it may seem odd to an adult mind, the paper itself can sometimes encourage a child to write. I fondly recall a little girl in my third-grade class who, at the mere presentation of a small, multi-colored writing tablet, would settle down to write a wonderful story. Usually, children do *not* like to write creatively on the yellow or green rough paper commonly provided for students in the lower grades. Instead they prefer nice, smooth, regular-sized paper. However, young children sometimes need lines to guide their manuscript printing. The teacher, with the aid of a ditto machine, can provide such a combination by using "nice" paper and putting lines on it lengthwise to allow more words on each line. Also available should be colored construction paper, lined ditto paper in various hues, drawing paper, charcoal paper, and easel paper. Additionally, a picture file of different illustrations is a "must." Some unusual pictures may often be just the stimulus a child needs to spark an idea for a new story.

If the Writing Center is suitably attractive, well stocked, organized, and inviting, children will be drawn toward it more and more often. Enthusiasm for writing, illustrating, and reading the works of other writers is contagious, and a "creative renaissance" in the classroom is begun.

Guiding the Writing Process

The number one objective of the Writing Center is to encourage children to write voraciously and unself-consciously. All that has been said thus far is to that end. However, it is obvious that the child must realize that proper spelling, punctuation, paragraphing, and other mechanical concerns of our language are of importance also. In an Affective Reading Program, that the child feels good about his or her work is of primary concern, and the mechanics are considered of secondary significance to the child's expressing him or herself freely. Therefore, the editing of a child's work should always be considered in a session entirely separate from the spontaneous, creative phase.

Prewriting. The first stage in the writing process is getting an idea, and some researchers suggest that more time should be spent in this phase than in later phases. This phase includes any experience, activity, or exercise that motivates a person to write. In the classroom the teacher may provide inspirational "prompts," such as story starters or visualization activities, or a discussion and resultant brainstorming session might lead to writing ideas. Another prewriting activity is "talking through" one's idea with a friend or small group.

Writing a Rough Draft. Even for professional adult writers, it is rarely possible to write a perfect finished product the first time through. The teacher must make it very clear to the children that this is in no way expected of them. With that in mind, it should be understood that the major portion of students' writing may be submitted in rough draft form and can be acknowledged as such. However, other works will be rewritten and polished, and then published. Work that is "published" is that which will be used for display and ceremoniously made public. Children should be made to realize that publishing need not occur with every piece of writing that they produce. Instead, it can be a special, celebrated event set aside for each child's most prized accomplishments. It should happen periodically for *every* child in the class.

Because they are the authors, the children themselves should have the final say in which of their creations will be reworked for publication. Children can be helped with their ability to evaluate by having them keep a personal file of all the writing they have done during the year. Upon rereading some of their earlier work, they may decide to select an almost forgotten creation to revise and publish. Or they may sometimes wish to write special pieces solely for the purpose of eventual publication. The teacher should always be available to make suggestions and to encourage children to publish the child's most creative and original works, but only if these opinions are expressly requested.

Responding. In this phase children share their piece with a trusted friend or peer editor. Children must be trained to give helpful feedback to their classmates, the more specific the better. This can be done through the use of a "response guide" where children are provided with sentence frames that they can use to help them to articulate appropriate responses. For example:

- Request for clarification: "Can you explain the part where . . .?"
- Appreciation: "I like the part where . . ." or "You used some good words, like . . ."
- Request for elaboration: "Can you tell me more about . . .?" or "How did you feel when . . .?"
  (Butler, 1991).

Revising. With the feedback from the peer editor, the child may now choose to reexamine, rethink, or resee his/her writing with a new insight into how the "audience" saw it. This phase may include changing the sequence of events, paragraphing, changing the voice used, or in similar ways attempting to communicate more fully.

Editing. Once it has been decided which story will be published, it is crucial to actively involve students in the initial stages of editing. In the creative process, the students were busily concentrating on getting their ideas on paper. But later they are often able to identify many of their own spelling or punctuation errors for editing purposes. During this phase, they might be encouraged to carefully read through their stories to correct all the mechanical errors they can find. Then stories can be traded with a trusted friend, who can point out and correct additional mistakes. Finally, the work is given to the teacher, who does NOT grade the work, but merely underlines misspelled words or grammatical errors, or circles letters that need not be capitalized. The student then makes the actual corrections.

The Writing Conference. After the child's mechanical errors have been corrected, a brief writing conference may be scheduled with the teacher. It is imperative to begin the conference on a positive note. The child's ideas may now be recognized and praised profusely. The teacher also lets the child know that their cooperative goal is to make the story even better, if possible.

Any structural changes, or expansions, can be suggested at this session. If expansion or clarification is needed, the child might be asked if (s)he can provide more information about a particular point. If the child is "stuck," the teacher may ask permission to help the child expand the idea(s).

Developing Skill with the Conventions of Writing. Through the writing conferences, the teacher has ample opportunity to perceive the areas in which his/her students need instruction. (S)he can, based upon this diagnostic information, devise "mini-lessons" for a small group, or in some cases the whole class, built around the childrens' needs. For example, the teacher might determine that the children are ready to learn about dialogue, flashbacks, or combining sentences, etc.

Once any expansions are completed, the child can be assisted in deciding where to divide the work into paragraphs. As students may soon be illustrating the things that happen in the story, they might be asked to reread their stories to determine which sentences would best fit together with one picture. Then they can be encouraged to look for groups of sentences that describe each event that occurs. Finally, they should be asked to draw a large "balloon" around those sentences that all go together. In this way children begin to discover naturally how cohesive paragraphs are formed.

Following is an example of a story (A) as it was originally conceived in rough draft form by a third-grade girl. Example B is the same story after the child, her peers, and the teacher have corrected the punctuation and spelling. During the writing conference, the story was expanded and put into paragraph form by the child, with assistance from the teacher.

Story A (rough draft)
Tasha

Tasha was a quite girl, she would never speak. Her freinds and family tryed and tryed to get her to speak. but she was vary bashful. The neibors always said is Tasha talking yet and Tasha mother would say no. Tasha loved beatiful cloths and every day she would walk dowtown to go to the big department store. One day she was at a big department store on the elavor and it stoped. It was stuck between floor so noone could get on or off the elevor. The people inside the elavor began to push and shuve. Tasha was shuved into a corner and she mothe for the frist time and screamed stop. Her scream was so lode the elevor started shaking. Then she started a earthquack. The earthquack shook the elavor back down to the ground. Noone ever asked Tasha to speak again.

Story B (corrected copy)

Tasha was a quiet girl. She would never speak. Her friends and family tried and tried to get her to speak, but she was very bashful. The neighbors always asked, "Is Tasha talking yet?" and Tasha's mother would sadly shake her head no.

Tasha loved beautiful clothes and every day she would walk downtown to the big department stores. Her favorite store was Lucy's, because it was twenty stories high.

One day Tasha was at Lucy's going up to the very top floor when—SCREECH!—the elevator stopped! It was stuck between floors so that no one could get on or off the elevator. The people inside the elevator began to push and shove. Tasha was shoved into a corner and she was getting squished. Finally, Tasha opened her mouth for the first time and screamed, "Stop!" Her scream was so loud that the elevator started shaking. Then the whole building started shaking. Then the *whole world* started shaking. Tasha had started an *earthquake*!

After ten minutes, the earthquake shook the elevator right back down to the ground. All the people were safe. The whole town heard about what Tasha had done and they *never* asked her to speak again!

Finally, the writing conference should always be a relaxed, "give and take" session where the child feels free to explain ideas that the teacher may not have understood and the child should feel at liberty to disagree with some of the teacher's recommendations. The teacher should bear in mind the following suggestions:

1) Be sensitive to the author's feelings and possible need for confidentiality.
2) Use the author's words, not yours. Be most concerned with "what" is said, rather than "how" it is said.
3) Make sure all comments take into consideration the age, ability level, and writing experience of the author.
4) Make all editorial comments in the presence of the author so (s)he has a chance to respond or explain.
5) Provide no letter or number grade. Evaluation should be in the form of constructive comments addressing the ideas of the story. At least one positive comment should always be made!

Making a Cover. The less "mentally taxing" activity of designing a cover for the story is sandwiched into the middle of the publishing process in order to give children a break from the tedious, and often difficult, work of editing. It also serves as an incentive to do the rewriting for the final, polished copy.

Elaborate techniques for binding may be used for the lengthier creations, but most children like the relative ease of using a large sheet of construction paper, folded over and eventually stapled, for their front covers. The art work for this outer leaf can be decorated with paint, tissue paper, torn construction paper, markers, or any of the other media contained in the Writing Center.

Children may be encouraged to show a favorite scene from their story on the cover, or one that is funny, exciting, or interesting to them. They might then choose a title that best captures the ideas in the writing, or one that would best entice other children to read it. Also, the author's full name can be included on the front cover. Actual book covers can be made available to children to demonstrate a variety of possible cover designs.

Finally, completed covers can be laminated with help from the teacher, art teacher, or librarian. Lamination helps to give the cover more substance and durability, and children seem to like the way it makes their cover look and feel—shiny and nice.

The Final Copy. It is this final step in the writing process that makes students feel they are actually "publishing." Every effort must be made to make the children's writing as much like "real books" as possible. Publishing houses do not use lined paper; therefore, for the final copy children may be given unlined 8 1/2" x 11" paper. To aid in neatness and "line control," they can be given "tracers" which should be placed underneath the unlined paper. A variety of structural styles might be offered so that the children can pick the ones that best fit the illustrations on each of their pages:

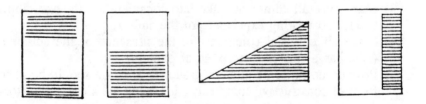

Publication. Supplying ample avenues for sharing their work is the most important key to making publication an exciting "reward" for children. The students have written down their ideas, illustrated their work and have paid all the meticulous attention to detail required of careful editing. Now they need recognition—lots of it! As each book is finished, it should be decorously brought to the attention of all the other children in the class. Plenty of praise should be given for the hard work completed, and abundant appreciation given for the particular merits of the literary effort. Children may then wish to read the book or have the teacher read the book aloud to the class. Eventually, the book should be displayed in a place of honor in the classroom. A comment sheet may be attached to the last page to allow other children to share their reactions and congratulate the author.

When all classmates have had a chance to review the book, the author may consent to read the book to other classes. Arrangements might be made to have a group of authors share their creations with others in the community, such as at a day care center or a nursing home. Finally, the child will want to bring the book home to share with proud parents, siblings, or other family members.

Thus positively reinforced, the author is typically eager to start the project over again, with the next idea that is captured on paper.

Summary

Most children will enjoy writing IF they are never forced to do so, and IF they are not made to write about something that is of no interest to them, and IF they are not immediately penalized for mechanics that are less than perfect.

Just as children select the books that they wish to read in an Affective Reading Program, so are they also free to write about whatever it is that is capturing their fancies at the moment. A child's wonderfully imaginative writing is a blend of thoughts and feelings released through the medium of words. The thoughts and feelings come from the child's own experiences, which can be first-hand, or sparked by books, television, pictures, movies, music, or any one of a number of things that fill their lives. Affective Reading is a truly whole-language approach to learning.

Sometimes a child will be tempted to write by first expressing his or her emotions through some artistic medium and then telling, in words, what it all means to them. Other children just like the crispness, color or variety of paper in the Writing Center so much that they are inspired to put their thoughts upon it. Of course, a few hesitant souls harbor doubts about whether they have anything at all worth saying. Soon, however, given the magic momentum of a "writing revolution" where other children are creating, illustrating, editing and finally publishing books to the celebration of the entire class, these reluctant children, too, begin to write.

At first the creative efforts of these children may be very feeble attempts. This is okay. Real growth only occurs when children begin to realize they cannot "fail." No admonishment is given for poor handwriting or faulty mechanics. No thoughts or ideas are ever ridiculed. Instead, a positive support system composed of the teacher and classmates makes it possible for every child to produce a finished product worth proudly sharing with the world.

References

Burrows, A.T., D.C. Jackson, and D.O. Saunders. (1964). *They All Want to Write: Written English in the Elementary School*. New York: Holt, Rinehart, and Winston.

Butler, S. (1991). "The Writing Connection." In V. Froese (ed.). *Whole-Language: Practice and Theory*. Boston: Allyn and Bacon.

Cowen, J.E. (1983). *Teaching Reading Through the Arts*. Newark: The International Reading Association.

Graves, D. (1985). *Breaking Ground: Teachers Relate Reading and Writing in the Elementary School*. Exeter, NH: Heinemann Educational Books.

Graves, D. (1983). *Writing: Teachers and Children at Work*. Exeter, NH: Heinemann.

Petty, W.T., and P.J. Finn, co-editors. (1975). *The Writing Processes of Students*. Buffalo: Report of the Annual Conference on Language Arts.

Sealey, L., N. Sealey, and M. Millmore. (1979). *Children's Writing: An Approach for the Primary Grades*. Newark: The International Reading Association.

Chapter 12

Reaching Culturally and Linguistically Diverse Learners

Recognition of the inherent dignity and of the equal and inalienable rights of all members of the human family is the foundation of freedom, justice and peace in the world.
—Universal Declaration of Human Rights

While once a teacher might have been able to expect a relatively homogeneous classroom filled with average, English-speaking, middle-class children, (s)he can now look forward to a heterogeneous garden of children with a diverse set of individual backgrounds. Every child will have a unique history and all will have interesting stories to tell; some stories will be very sad. The inordinate amount of stresses on children may range from young immigrants eagerly facing a new life in a strange and often inhospitable culture, to extreme poverty and despair.

Indeed, more than ever, an Affective Reading Program is needed to offer a nurturing environment for learning how to read and write. Krashen (1985) talks about an "Affective Filter" that implies that high anxiety, low motivation and low self-confidence will create a negative affective state in which children who are trying to learn a second language will be much less likely to succeed. To spring open this affective filter, teachers need to use some special affective strategies and must be especially sensitive to the background of their learners. Let's look at a couple of examples.

Sione, age six, arrives from Tonga. He misses breadfruit and poi, he misses his cousins and friends, but perhaps most of all he misses the ease with which he could express himself in the Tongan language and make others understand. To Sione's new first-grade teacher, Tonga is only a name—it is not even a spot on the map, let alone a language and a culture. Both Sione and the teacher try to gesture to each other, but it doesn't work very well.

119

Maria, age eight, comes to the United States from Mexico understanding only a few broken phrases of English which her family has picked up in a few weeks of trying to shop in the local grocery store. The words sound harsh, crude, and threatening, as her black eyes dart quickly around the classroom, desperately trying to pick up some clue as to what is being said. Maria is placed in a regular third-grade classroom so that she may have an opportunity to interact socially with American children her own age. Her teacher has had no instruction or experience with the Spanish language. The look in the teacher's eyes when Maria breaks into desperate Spanish is as blank as the look on Maria's shy, bewildered face.

So is it possible for a monolingual teacher with little background in world cultures to successfully cope with the needs of a child who is struggling with a new home and a new language? The answer is an enthusiastic "yes," and fortunately many of the strategies that have proven effective in helping second-language learners are the very components and variations of an affective, whole language approach to literacy instruction. Such instruction will benefit not only the child who is learning English, but her/his native English-speaking classmates as well.

The Environment Must Be Conducive to Language Acquisition

For any language to be acquired, it must be practiced constantly; a child who is struggling to learn a new language must be provided with ample opportunities for risk-free experimentation and affirming feedback. Conversation and discussion in the child's language and in English—or in some combination of the two—must not only be tolerated, but encouraged. All children must feel free to ask questions when they do not understand something and those questions must be treated with respect by the teacher and the other students. The teacher must ask questions that require thinking and language beyond a "yes" or "no" response, and children must be given sufficient time to formulate their responses. Children like Maria and Sione must understand that their ideas are more important to the teacher and the other students than the words they use to articulate them, and that their teacher and classmates will respect them for what they think and not judge them for how their words are put together. Sione and Maria must be led to understand, for example, that their understanding and appreciation of nature are a contribution they can make to their classmates, just as their classmates' understanding of English and technology will eventually make a contribution to them.

Grouping for Success

Because the second-language learner is often hesitant to speak before a large group, cooperative partnerships and small-group projects that will require some verbal interaction are particularly helpful. The teacher is in the ideal position to recognize the individual talents that children possess and to offer praise and encouragement for what children CAN contribute rather than calling attention to what they CANNOT do. When a teacher assigns a small group task, for example, (s)he can mention to the entire class exactly what abilities it will take in order for the group to be successful at the task. For example, Komae, from Japan, may have a good eye for design. Although she is hesitant to talk when the entire class is listening, because her sentences still come out awkwardly, she will take the initiative when she, José and Dan are working on a poster advertising the book *Island of the Blue Dolphin.* José speaks no English at all, but he immediately gets to work painting the background for the display. When this task is completed, the teacher has the opportunity to specifically recognize—and publicly assign status—to all the children in the group. This is done by bringing to the attention of the class the skills that were demonstrated in making the poster display and how important each child, including the non-English speaker and the limited-English speaker, were to the successful completion of the task the group was assigned. Such a strategy is called the "multiple ability treatment" and was developed by Tammivaara (1982) to help to modify the negative expectations that children sometimes hold for classmates who differ from themselves.

Alternate Modes of Expression

Many children for whom speaking English is still a struggle can express their understanding of concepts through a variety of ways. Dance, murals, art projects, and creative drama have tremendous value in an Affective Reading Program. Pantomime, which requires body but not oral language, helps to build confidence that will pave the way for further class participation. Maria, with her sensitivity and natural agility, may be given another way in which she can gain the respect of her classmates. In a role play activity, Sione can be a soccer coach who lets his players do most of the talking; then with a few carefully chosen words and a demonstration, *he* steps in and solves the problem. Choral reading is another mode of expression that is helpful to second-language learners. Such a group reading activity is nonthreatening because it provides an opportunity to practice pronunciation without worrying about content or structure, and one's mistakes are noticeable only to oneself.

Making Books Accessible

Teachers in today's classrooms are moving away from traditional ability grouping. While this move is positive in that it avoids stigmatizing children placed in the "slowest" reading groups (as was too often the fate of the culturally and linguistically diverse learner) it also means that such children are often faced with books that are too difficult for them. To make such books accessible to second-language learners, Fielding and Roller (1992) make these suggestions:

1. *Allow plenty of time for self-selected reading.* This part of an Affective Reading Program is especially critical for second-language learners because such unstructured contacts with books are positive, even if the books are not "read" in the traditional sense. The pictures and a general sense of the gist of the story may lead to further interest in the content. The teacher can slip in comic books in a corner of the classroom library; it is easier for children to understand the words in these books because of the vivid context provided by the pictures, and the stories are humorous and fun. Wordless books, too, provide a way for children to tell stories in their own language, using the pictures and sequence to create text.

2. *Provide an easier book with the same content.* If a child's interests are in sports, for example, but the book the child selects is too difficult for him/her, supplying an easier book on the same topic can be an important precursor. The child picks up important vocabulary and concepts and is then ready—and motivated—to read the harder book.

3. *Provide a partner for the child.* A child who is just beginning to speak English can be paired with a fluent English speaker who is an able reader. Both children can be asked to share reactions to what is read verbally or pictorially. The limited-English speaker, after listening to the story and observing the illustrations, can be encouraged to retell the story in his/her native language.

4. *Allow the child to reread the book.* To gain fluency in English and to comprehend the material more fully, limited-English speakers benefit from repeated readings of a story. To make this a more interesting task, the child can reread the story into a tape recorder, or the child can be asked to "polish" up his/her performance to read to younger children.

5. *Read to children.* This cornerstone of an Affective Reading Program is the ultimate strategy for second-language learners because it increases understanding of vocabulary while exposing children to

standard English in a positive way. Also, as with all children, being read to is a "no fail" way to be exposed to a wide variety of literary genres and nonfictional topics. Finally, when the teacher reads and rereads a predictable book like Bill Martin's *Brown Bear, Brown Bear, What Do You See?*, Sione and Maria may not understand every word, but from the teachers' animation and the other children's participation and laughter, they can follow the general pattern of the story and begin to appreciate the flow of the language. As the two children chime in with the familiar rhymes and repetitive phrases, the two limited-English speakers begin to chime in too. These words and phrases soon become part of the growing reserve of English words which the two children can use more and more readily.

The First Few Days in the Classroom

The first few days in the classroom are, of course, the most difficult for the second-language learner. The teacher can help to ease such a child into the new classroom situation by pairing the newcomer with a friendly, compassionate child who will act as a "buddy" and guide. At the beginning, Maria and her buddy, Chrissy, might have to rely on smiles, gestures, and body language in order to pool their ingenuity in working a jigsaw puzzle together, but soon the words that have been an accompaniment to the gestures become the dominant means of communication; the gestures become a private joke between the two children. As Sione is drawn into a playground ball game by his buddy, Dan, he listens to the exclamations and shouts of the boys and tries out what he hears, watching Dan's face for the approval that will assure him that he has used the words somewhat appropriately.

The classroom and its routine need to be specially prepared for the second-language learner. Most classrooms are filled with pictures, cutouts, posters and bulletin board displays. To help familiarize the child with written as well as spoken language, the teacher of a second-language learner may add small placards labeling all pictures and displays as well as more mundane objects such as the chairs, desks, and the drinking fountain. Since survival during the school day depends on vital phrases such as "May I go to the restroom?" or "It's time for lunch," Sione's teacher may print these phrases on flash cards that Sione and Dan can practice as a game. Many minor crises can be avoided in the way!

Teachers in an Affective Reading Program must resist the temptation to occupy the newcomer with artificial, rather meaningless workbook pages while they work with the rest of the class. Instead, they must invite the children to be an important part of the class by using visual reinforcement and concrete examples to supplement as many of their verbal explanations as possible. Though it may be difficult, they need to use these visual representations to engage the second-language learners into discussions, so that they begin to listen, absorb, and feel free to practice new words and phrases as they encounter them.

Finally, to make the second-language learner feel especially welcome, the teacher can bring in a speaker of the child's language to broaden the other children's perspectives. Not only can the visitor introduce the child's language, but the speaker can share ideas, values, and customs from his/her culture (Tiedt & Tiedt, 1990). Similarly, the child him/herself can teach his/her classmates some phrases in his/her language, a song, and perhaps bring in a native food for his/her classmates to sample. For additional interest, the teacher can bring in excellent children's stories that reflect the culture of the child, such as *Juanita*, by Leo Politi, that gives the flavor of Mexican culture.

Developing Fluency

As the second-language learner becomes more comfortable in the new classroom and is beginning to pick up key words and phrases, the teacher needs to provide more and more complex opportunities for the child to interact verbally with the rest of the class. As the child experiments with the new language, the teacher must stringently avoid openly correcting the child, instead modeling the correct language patterns by elaborating upon the child's own statements. For example, if Maria brings her new doll for show and tell and announces, "Look! I bring my doll school today!", the teacher might affirm her statement by responding, "Oh, you *brought* your new doll to school today?" The teacher may use a similar technique to help the child with English transformations that can be very difficult for the emergent English speaker. When Sione exclaims, "There be four pencils on my desk," the teacher would reply, "Yes, Sione, there are four pencils on your desk! How many pencils are on Hoa's desk?"

In a more formalized context, affective teachers of reading may want to use a flannelboard activity to allow children to respond to literature in their own words. This approach uses visual aids to focus children's attention on the most important ideas in the story and helps them to follow the sequence from the context of the aids. For example, *The Gingerbread Man* would begin with a general discussion about running away. Has any one of them ever run away from something or someone? Then the teacher would read the story and illustrate the action in sequence by putting tagboard figures of the old woman, gingerbread boy, the cat, the bird, the fox, etc. on the flannelboard adhered by velcro glued onto their backs. Predictive questions are interspersed throughout the reading of the story. At the culmination of the story, small groups are invited to recite the story in their own words—or in their own language—using the visual aids.

The emphasis in all reading and writing activities in an Affective Reading Program with second-language learners should be on *function* rather than on form: that is, *what* is said rather than how it is said. The teacher must realize that a child's pronunciation, grammar, and accent will correct themselves with time, practice, and immersion in standard English. The teacher's task is to model standard English, to listen carefully to the child's ideas in whatever form they may take, and to celebrate the child's attempts to communicate.

Summary

A child who is struggling to learn English as a second language and to adjust to the American culture and way of life has a great chance for success if he/she is placed in an Affective Reading Program where the teacher and students are accepting of personal differences; where ideas and opinions are openly and frequently expressed; where a variety of multicultural and multiethnic literature is presented through oral reading, silent reading, choral reading, and creative drama; and where teacher and students are oriented toward ideas, feelings, and personal visions, rather than formalities in expressing them. In short, the child needs an environment that is visually stimulating, linguistically enriched, and emotionally warm and accepting. The teacher need not speak fluent Spanish or Tongan to help Maria and Sione to have a successful school experience. Awareness of a few techniques, willingness to put forth a little effort, and compassion to understand and to care—these are the prerequisites. Any teacher can achieve them.

References

Fielding, L., and C. Roller. (1992). "Making Difficult Books Accessible and Easy Books Acceptable." *The Reading Teacher* 45, (9), 678-685.

Krashen, S.D. (1985). *Inquiries & Insights: Second Language Teaching: Immersion & Bilingual Education: Literacy*. Hayward, CA: Alemany Press.

Tammivaara, J. (1982). "The Effects of Task Structure on the Beliefs about Competence and Participation in Small Groups." *Sociology of Education*, 55, 212-222.

Tiedt, P.L. and I.M. Tiedt. (1990). *Multicultural Teaching: A Handbook of Activities, Information and Resources*. Boston: Allyn and Bacon.

Chapter Thirteen

Basic "Truths" in Teaching Children: What is Negotiable

A prime factor in the ability to rise to the challenge of freedom is the desire to do so. Yet the belief is widespread, even among educators, that most teachers relish the security of knowing in detail what is expected of them and how they are expected to do it.

—Richard Renfield,
If Teachers Were Free

A sensitive teacher who has carefully read the preceding pages may still be trying to come to terms with how to fit such an innovative, full program into his or her own classroom. A teacher may have to contend with a prescribed basal reading program, a limited time allotment for reading and language arts, a scarcity of funds for materials, a rigidly mandated curriculum, or an administration that does not seem amenable to any changes at all. These barriers, or ones similar to them, are unfortunate realities in many classroom situations. But they need not cause the teacher to despair of ever teaching affectively!

For the host of teachers finding themselves in such a quandary as they reach the end of this book, I have chosen to provide a broad second look at the Affective Reading Program in terms of current research, and in terms of what my own teaching experience tells me is most important: just which factors in any reading program are arbitrary in nature—or "negotiable"? In other words, which factors are not for the experts to decide and define, but should be left for each individual teacher to come to terms with him or herself?

Negotiable Factors

Consider the following four scenarios:

In one first-grade classroom, the children are reading a story about a fight that recently took place on the playground. They will soon copy the story to put in a cumulative book they have been writing all year.

In another classroom a list of one-syllable words each containing the short "i" sound are presented on the board: "Tim," "thin," "his," "is," "ill," "win," and "bid." Later the children will read from their basals: "Tim is thin. Will thin Tim win his bid? Tim will."

A group of second-graders are reading books they have selected from the classroom library. Several other students in the class are creating a skit based on a book that all in the group have read. Another small group is painting a mural depicting the sequential events in a book that was read to them.

In yet a fourth classroom, seemingly unrelated new vocabulary is presented to children on flash cards. Then the teacher asks the children if they have ever lost a pet. She is motivating the children in the group to read a story about a missing puppy.

Method of Teaching. The majority of the students in the above examples will more than likely learn to read, even though they are being instructed by widely disparate methods. One may argue interminably about the relative merits (or demerits) of each approach. But the fact is that research over the past twenty years has continually supported a conclusion that it is the teacher—not the method of instruction—who determines whether or not the students will learn to read (Weintraub, et al., 1980; Smith, 1978; Bond and Tinker, 1973; Bond and Dykstra, 1976). As a matter of fact, we are teaching children the mechanics of reading better than ever today! The issue at hand is that teachers now need to concentrate their efforts on getting children who HAVE the ability to read DOING so because they see it as an enjoyable, personally rewarding thing to do (Blair and Turner, 1985).

Additionally, that the "majority" learns to read subtly suggests that with *any* of the above methods a few children manage to "slip through the cracks." These unfortunate individuals may not learn to read at all. Therefore, a comprehensive reading program must consist of a variety of appealing methods if one is to address the needs of each learner. But exactly *which* combination of methods used may not be of the most earthshaking importance and is best left to the discretion of each individual teacher.

The Physical Environment. Hundreds of books containing cute bulletin board ideas are published for teachers each year, along with other novel ideas for room decoration. Preservice teachers are continually cautioned in college methods courses that desks arranged in neat, traditional rows are passé. Moreover, attractive-looking interest and learning centers are touted as the only possible way to cure the classroom "blahs."

Yet I once knew a teacher who taught in the inner city in a classroom that had been converted from an old storage closet. The room was exceedingly cramped, lacked adequate light and ventilation, and the desks and chairs were in absolute disrepair. The students in that class, however, had an incredible "esprit de corps." It was obvious they felt that they were the smartest, most special children in the whole world. All this was mostly due to a dynamic, caring teacher who saw her mission as the educating of impressionable young human beings. Her vision went far beyond the superficial "window dressing" of more prosperous classrooms.

Another teacher professed a complete lack of artistic or creative ability. His classroom had a noticeable lack of attractive bulletin boards, or any of the plethora of colorful displays one usually finds in an elementary classroom. But at any given time, one could enter that room and find a lively discussion going on, with respectful give and take between teacher and students. At other times students would be sitting cross-legged on the floor reading to themselves and each other while the teacher held individual reading conferences.

No doubt there *is* merit in having an appealing, nicely decorated classroom. But the bottom line here is best expressed by an old adage: "Beauty is only skin deep." In other words, those things which are *most* crucial in making a positive classroom environment, where students feel good about themselves and are eager to learn, run deeper than the mere physical trappings. Moreover, if a teacher does not feel comfortable with or philosophically committed to more "progressive" room arrangements, (s)he should stick to what feels best. The teacher should bear in mind that the "emotional" environment is more important than the "physical" one. It is a positive emotional environment that creates children who are capable and eager to learn.

Grading Systems. The reporting of students' grades is, historically, a controversial issue. When "permissive" educators in the sixties proposed that grading be abolished entirely to take pressure off slower students, arguments ensued. Equally impassioned "traditionalists" countered: How will those students who try hard and achieve well be rewarded? How would we ever be able to discriminate between the "good" and the "poor" students when it is time to decide who should go to college? And how would the "under- achievers" begin to realize they had better start trying harder?

Some school systems got around the whole issue by dropping grades in favor of anecdotal comments. When some teachers complained it was too taxing to think of original comments to describe every child's progress, standard comments were numbered, so that a simple digit could stand for any conceivable comment a teacher might have about the child's work in any subject. Of course, the comments were not quantifiable, so many teachers, as well as parents, felt uncomfortable without the ability to report progress in ways that had relative numerical value.

As an example of the overemphasis placed on grades, I recall a very long and volatile faculty meeting where the sole item on the agenda was whether to assign letter grades, as had been done in the past, or to adopt a system of pluses and minuses, as other schools in the area were doing. Such a small point over which to waste time and strong emotions!

The heart of the issue is this: whatever the grading system used, remember that *children* are being graded, not cattle or chickens. Always give the child the benefit of the doubt. Any system can be used constructively to help children recognize their progress and note their improvement. However, a child should *never* feel devastated by a report card, whether it is due to an "F," an "F+," or a "Jason talks too much in class." There should *always* be something positive for the child to be proud of on the report, whether it is a personal comment praising the child's ability to make paper swans, or a grade showing outstanding improvement in reading.

Methods of Discipline. In a highly motivational program that strives to reach every learner on an emotional level, the need for discipline is greatly reduced. It might be said in this regard that the emphasis in an Affective Reading Program is on "prevention" rather than "cure." Instead of worrying about what one should do when a child misbehaves, the teacher concentrates on really making the program exciting to all children. In this way, students are very busily engaged in the task at hand and are less likely to get into mischief. They are continually praised for the things they do "right" rather than punished for what they do "wrong." In addition, adequate provision is made for the academic and emotional needs of children with lesser ability. This helps the "slower" children to gain the attention they need by their positive accomplishments rather than their misdeeds.

However, in any classroom there are times when children may need to understand that their behavior at that moment is inappropriate. There are a multitude of commonly used techniques for humanely dealing with minor disciplinary infractions. While my own classroom disruptions seemed to be best alleviated by a quick and private word to the perpetrator, I have seen a variety of other tactics used effectively by different teachers. Some withdrew a classroom privilege; others had the child sign a written agreement with the teacher stating that the misbehavior would not happen again.

The most important factor to consider in this issue is, again, that it is not the method, but the way that the discipline is handled by the teacher that determines its effectiveness. If maintaining the child's dignity is *always* the chief concern, any recourse will be followed fairly, lovingly, and consistently. The child will be led to understand that it was the isolated act that was disapproved of, and not the child.

Instructional Materials. For the first teaching job interview that I ever attended, the principal asked me, "If you were asked to teach aboard a jetliner with only trade books, pencils and paper, and a chalkboard, could you succeed?" At the time, it seemed an odd question, for I knew the classrooms in his school were full of textbooks, teaching machines, and supplementary material. Over the years, however, I have decided that it was a very wise question. Those basic materials *should* be all that an enthusiastic and creative teacher needs to promote learning, although a wide selection of materials provides variety for the children and makes the teacher's job a great deal easier.

As far as *which* materials to choose, the simple answer is "whatever the teacher feels most comfortable with, and those that (s)he has found the students like and respond to best." Teachers are literally swamped with catalogues from publishers of commercial materials, as well as basal reader salespersons. These folks confidently assure the teacher that their material is the *only* material that could possibly teach children to read. This is nonsense! The majority of materials from reputable publishers have been devised by experts in the field of reading and are field-tested by large groups of children before they ever appear on the market. Nearly *all* offer something.

To the extent that they provide novelty to a program and motivation for some children, teaching machines (such as the controlled reader or a computer) may be worthwhile, although they have not been found to obtain better gains in achievement than more teacher-directed materials. However, if the teacher is excited about reading machines, that enthusiasm will be transferred to the students.

The key issue is that teachers should choose the materials that they feel work best to motivate their students to read. If a limited budget is available for reading, however, that money might better be spent on a selection of books—as these are the real "stuff" of reading—rather than for purchasing machines or paraphernalia that has less direct association with usual reading patterns.

Non-negotiable Factors

While there are many ways to excel at being an affective teacher, there are certain traits which are indeed NON-negotiable; that is, every teacher should be exemplifying them. Their existence epitomizes the essence of what is meant by an "affective teacher."

Being There. Every school system offers teachers a number of "personal days" and an even larger number of "sick days." These days are certainly a safety valve of sorts, so that teachers are not unnecessarily penalized when they are truly sick or encounter emergency situations. However, a number of teachers feel these days are part of their fringe benefits and thus use them indiscriminately, calling them "rest and relaxation" or R&R days. If such teachers only knew how they are missed by the children—particularly those poor souls for whom the teacher/student relationship is their only lifeline—they might reconsider their choice! For many, many children of trauma, who more and more populate our schools, it is a sad, wasted day when the teacher, with whom they have bonded, is not in school.

Safe Environment. Another non-negotiable item is that the teacher must strive for an environment that is safe for every child. By "safe" I mean that there is never any fear of ridicule or abuse, certainly not from the teacher, but also simply not accepted from other children. Moreover, the environment must be so safe that children feel free to ask and answer questions and make comments—and know they will be affirmed for doing so. The environment must be a fertile one for all children to take emotional and academic risks.

Celebrate Diversity. Decades ago, children were expected to come to school, forget their native language, and assimilate into American culture as rapidly as possible. America was considered a "melting pot" where cultural differences were considered a limitation (Tiedt & Tiedt, 1990). Today the presence of cultural diversity is considered a strength and we like to think of our country more as a "tossed salad," where various cultural groups can contribute to the national culture while still keeping their language and discrete cultural identity. Pride in ethnic heritage should be actively fostered in an affective classroom, and diversity celebrated, as one celebrates the variety of flowers in one's garden.

Love and Respect. In a nutshell, the affective teacher is one who demonstrates boundless love and respect for his/her students. This trait is not only non-negotiable, but it is *the* definitive feature of an affective teacher and program.

Summary

Because the Affective Reading Program has been prescribed in considerable detail, some teachers may worry that conflicts within their existing school situations may prohibit a faithful replication of such a program.

This chapter has been an attempt to put such fears to rest. It has briefly discussed the large and often controversial issues of methods, physical environment, grades, discipline, and instructional materials. In the proposed reading program, these factors are "negotiable" and it is felt that they are best left to the discretion of a competent teacher.

Those factors which are *not* negotiable in an Affective Reading Program should not make a good teacher lose hope of ever implementing such a program in his or her classroom. They cost nothing. They won't unduly upset the administration. They take nothing away from the existing curriculum; indeed, they enhance it. In fact, they can be used in *all* programs in *all* classrooms, for they concern the teacher and his or her relationship with the students. They are the factors of love and respect for the children, and an understanding that high motivation is *the* pivotal element in all learning.

These are the non-negotiable factors that make the program truly affective, and they are the "heart" of this book.

References

Blair, T.R., and E.C. Turner. (1985). "Ideal and Real World of Recreational Reading," *Journal of Reading Education*, 10, no. 2: 15-21.

Bond, G.L., and R. Dykstra. (1967). *Final Report of the Coordinating Center for First-Grade Reading Instruction* (USOE Project x-0001).

Bond, G.L., and M.A. Tinker. (1973). *Reading Difficulties: Their Diagnosis and Correction*. Englewood Cliffs, NJ: Prentice-Hall.

Brophy, J.E., and C.M. Evertson. (1976). *Learning from Teaching: A Developmental Perspective*. Boston: Allyn and Bacon.

Brubaker, D.L. (1976). *Creative Leadership in Elementary Schools*. Dubuque: Kendall/Hunt.

Chamberlin, J.G. (1981). *The Educating Act: A Phenomenological View*. Washington, D.C.: University Press of America.

Renfield, R. (1969). *If Teachers Were Free*. New York: Dell Publishing Company.

Smith, F. (1978). *Reading Without Nonsense*. New York: Teachers' College Press.

Tiedt, P.L., and I.M. Tiedt. (1990). *Multicultural Teaching: A Handbook of Activities, Information and Resources*. Boston: Allyn and Bacon.

Weintraub, S., S. Rosen, N. Rowe, and W. Hill. (1980). *Annual Summary of Investigations Related to Reading*. Newark, Del.: IRA.

Afterword

From my own experience teaching in the elementary grades, one thing became increasingly clear: all teaching needs to be directed toward the "heart" of the learner in order for real learning to take place. Learning must be fun in order for it to be really received at all. Now, "fun" in a child's world does not have to mean the opposite of "work" as an adult would understand the terms. Absolutely not! To children, it can mean pride and the feeling of accomplishment of having participated in an amiable group, of having added something important to that group, and of feeling real satisfaction because you are a better person for having been in the group. "Fun" can be directly related to the feeling of being accepted and belonging. It means that you spend your time in a way that is meaningful to you so that you feel pleased with your own work.

"Fun," to a child, can also be hard work. It can be writing, illustrating, and editing a book. It can be a bunch of fifth-graders perspiring profusely as they hammer the finishing touches on to the witch's roof for the play *Hansel and Gretel*. Or it can be a second-grader contorting his little face so hard that the teacher wonders if it will break, while trying to sound out a word in a book he has chosen to read. Or fun can even be a sixth-grader "burning the midnight oil" to finish the last book in the *Little House on the Prairie* series.

An Affective Reading Program is the way to make reading and learning fun. Rather than incidental references to motivating children, motivation is *the* focus of this entire reading program. Because not all individuals find the same activities fun and exciting, the program consists of several kinds of reading components that complement one another and combine to form the most comprehensive and enjoyable whole language program possible.

None of the individual programs are new. But each provides something so vital that the whole becomes much more dynamic than the sum of its parts. A self-selected reading component allows children to freely practice the skills of reading with materials that are of the most interest to them. Children are not bored by unnecessary drills on skills, but are grouped temporarily when skill assistance is needed. Each child's progress is monitored by the teacher, as well as by the child.

Enhancement of reading experiences is provided by writing, performing, and doing other activities that are also of the child's choosing.

Beginning reading is started with the Language Experience Approach, for it alone allows children to read the words that are the most meaningful to them and then create stories from their own childlike world view. The approach moves from the whole to its parts: the child reads his/her story and then learns to analyze the "building blocks" of stories—the letters and words.

From the beginning, too, children write their own individual creative stories, just because they have things to say. Inspired perhaps by their own artwork or a picture in a book, they feel free to write down their innermost thoughts and their whimsical ideas. They are helped to edit the stories they like best, with their teacher and classmates' help, for the purpose of publication.

Poetry, also, has its place in the Affective Reading Program, because it is so natural a vent for the fantasies of a child. Children are inspired by the poetry of other children and are then given formulas to increase their confidence as budding poets. Children become free, through poetry, to be silly, or "crazy," or untruthful, or even to make dreams become reality.

Cloze certainly belongs in such a program, because it helps children to become aware of the power words can give them. By using cloze exercises faithfully, children feel the exhilaration of finding, from their own minds, the right words for a sentence so that it says *just exactly* what they want it to say.

Children develop the confidence to perform before others in the drama component, in which they initially read prepared scripts, but they soon advance to expressing their own ideas in skit format. Everyone in the class has a chance to "thrill to the applause of an audience," just as all have participated in creating, casting, and blocking the play.

Another important ingredient in the Affective Reading Program is the Read Aloud time, which makes effective use of any left over minutes, or even seconds, in the school day. Everything from lists of world records to popular song lyrics are read often to children to expand their experiences, broaden their interests, and to develop a warm and intimate bond that comes from sharing reading.

Finally, the program calls for the joining of forces between the teacher and the parents. Though the teacher, with his or her expertise, is the recognized "prime mover" of the program, maximum cooperation between the most important people in the child's life is stressed. Parents are encouraged to assist the child in reading in direct ways, such as listening to and praising the child's reading, and in indirect ways, such as modeling reading behavior and taking the child to the library.

These are the essential components which, in the hands of a competent and caring teacher, form a reading program which has the best chance of producing children who *can* and *do* read far beyond the classroom doors. There is a definite need in today's reading programs to kindle in children a real desire to read. The Affective Reading Program is the direct answer to this need.

Suggested Classroom Library for an
Affective Reading Program—K-6

W = Wordless Book   B = Beginner Book
PO = Poetry   P = Picture Story Book
        I = Intermediate (4-6)

Aardema, Verna. (1975). *Why Mosquitoes Buzz in People's Ears.* Illustrated by Leo and Diane Dillon. Dial. (P)

Alexander, Martha. (1970). *Bobo's Dream.* Illustrated by author. Dial. (W)

Alexander, Martha. (1971). *Nobody Asked Me If I Wanted a Baby Sister.* Illustrated by author. Dial. (P)

Alexander, Sally Hobart. (1990). *Mom Can't See Me.* Photographs by George Ancona. Macmillan. (B)

Allen, Pamela. (1980). *Mr. Archimedes' Bath.* Illustrated by author. Lothrop. (P)

Andersen, Hans Christian. (1953). *The Steadfast Tin Soldier.* Illustrated by Martha Brown. Scribner's. (P)

Anderson, Clarence. (1962). *Billy and Blaze.* Macmillan. (P)

Anderson, Joy. (1986). *Juma and the Magic Jinn.* Illustrated by Charles Mikolaycak. Lothrop, Lee & Shepard. (I).

Anno, Mitsumasa. (1982). *Anno's Britain.* Philomel. (W)

Ardizzone, Edward. (1970). *The Wrong Side of the Bed.* Doubleday. (W)

Armstrong, William H. (1970). *Sounder.* Harper. (I)

Aruego, Jose. (1971). *Look What I Can Do.* Scribner's. (W)

138

Bell, Clare. (1985). *Ratha's Creature*. Atheneum. (I)

Bemelmans, Ludwig. (1930). *Madeline*. Illustrated by author. Viking. (P)

Benchley, Nathaniel. (1969). *Sam the Minute Man*. Harper. (B)

Bergman, Tamar. (1988). *The Boy from Over There*. Translated from Hebrew by Hillel Helkin. Houghton Mifflin. (I)

Bierhorst, John, reteller. (1987). *Doctor Coyote: Native American Aesop's Fables*. Illustrated by Wendy Watson. Macmillan. (I)

Blake, Quentin. (1985). *The Story of the Dancing Frog*. Illustrated by author. Knopf. (I)

Bonsall, Crosby. (1974). *The Case of the Cat's Meow*. Harper. (B)

Bunting, Eve. (1989). *The Wednesday Surprise*. Illustrated by Donald Carrick. Clarion. (P)

Byars, Betsy. (1986). *The Golly Sisters Go West*. Illustrated by Sue Truesdell. Harper & Row. (P)

Carle, Eric. (1971). *Do You Want To Be My Friend?* Crowell. (W)

Carreno, Mada, reteller. (1987). *El Viaje del Joven Matsua (The Travels of the Youth Matsua)*. Illustrated by Gerardo Suzan. Trillas. (P)

Ciardi, John. (1985). *Doodle Soup*. Illustrated by Merle Nacht. Houghton Mifflin. (PO)

Coerr, Eleanor. (1988). *Chang's Paper Pony*. Illustrated by Deborah Kogan Ray. Harper & Row. (P)

Cohen, Caron Lee. (1988). *The Mud Pony*. Illustrated by Shonto Begay. Scholastic. (P)

Collier, James Lincoln. (1987). *Louis Armstrong*. Macmillan. (I)

Cooney, Barbara. (1982). *Miss Rumphius*. Illustrated by author. Viking. (P)

Curry, Jane Louise, reteller. (1987). *Back in the Beforetime: Tales of the California Indians*. Illustrated by James Wats. Macmillan. (I)

Dahl, Roald. (1966). *Charlie and the Chocolate Factory*. Harper. (I)

Dahl, Roald. (1964). *James and the Giant Peach*. Harper. (I)

Dalgliesh, Alice. (1954). *The Courage of Sarah Noble*. Illustrated by Leonard Weisgard. Charles Scribner's Sons. (P,I)

Davis, Deborah. (1989). *The Secret of the Seal*. Illustrated by Judy Labrasca. Crown. (P)

Delton, Judy. (1974). *Two Good Friends*. Crown. (B)

DeJong, Meindert. (1956). *The House of Sixty Fathers*. Illustrated by Maurice Sendak. Harper. (I)

DePaola, Tomie. (1973). *Nana Upstairs and Nana Downstairs*. Putnam. (P)

DePaola, Tomie. (1983). *The Legend of the Blue Bonnet*. Illustrated by author. Scholastic. (P)

DeTrivino, Elizabeth Borton. (1965). *I, Juan de Pareja*. Farrar Straus & Giroux. (I)

Eastman, P.D. (1961). *Go, Dog, Go!* Random House. (B)

Esbensen, Barbara Juster. (1988). *The Star Maiden*. Illustrated by Helen K. Davie. Little, Brown. (P)

Ets, Maria Hall. (1963). *Gilberto and the Wind*. Viking. (P)

Felton, Harold W. (1970). *Mumbet*. Illustrated by Donn Albright. Dodd, Mead & Co. (I)

Field, Rachel. (1964). *Listen, Rabbit*. Illustrated by Symeon Shimin. T. Crowell. (PO)

Fox, Paula. (1988). *The Village by the Sea*. Illustrated by author. Orchard Books. (I)

Friese, Kai. (1989). *Tenzin Gyatso, the Dalai Lama*. Illustrated by author. Chelsea. (I)

Fritz, Jean. (1982). *Homesick: My Own Story*. Illustrated by Margot Tomes. Putnam. (P,I)

Fuchs, Erich. (1969). *Journey to the Moon*. Delacorte. (W)

George, Jean Craighead. (1972). *Julie of the Wolves*. Harper. (I)

George, Jean Craighead. (1990). *On the Far Side of the Mountain*. Illustrated by author. E.P. Dutton. (I)

Ghermann, Beverly. (1991). *Sandra Day O'Connor: Justice for All*. Illustrated by Robert Masheris. Viking. (I)

Giovanni, Nikki. (1974). *Ego-Tripping and Other Poems for Young People*. Illustrated by George Ford. Lawrence Hill. (PO)

Goble, Paul, reteller. (1988). *Iktomi and the Boulder: A Plains Indian Story*. Illustrated by reteller. Orchard Books. (P)

Goldin, Barbara Diamond. (1991). *Cakes and Miracles: A Purim Tale*. Illustrated by Erika Weihs. Viking. (I)

Goodall, Jane. (1988). *My Life with the Chimpanzees*. Minstrel. (I)

Greenfield, Eloise. (1981). *Daydreamers*. Illustrated by Tom Feelings. Dial. (PO)

Greenfield, Eloise. (1988). *Honey, I Love, and Other Love Poems*. Harper & Row. (PO)

Gray, Nigel. (1989). *A Country Far Away*. Illustrated by Phillippe Dupasquier. Watts/Orchard Books. (P)

Griffith, Helen. (1975). *Just a Dog*. Holiday. (B)

Gripe, Maria. (1990). *Agnes Cecilia*. Translated from the Swedish by Rika Lesser. Harper. (I)

Guilfoile, Elizabeth. (1975). *Nobody Listens to Andrew*. Follett. (B)

Haley, Gail, adapter. (1970). *A Story: An African Tale*. Illustrated by adapter. Atheneum. (P)

Haven, Susan. (1990). *Is It Them or Is It Me?* Putnam. (I)

Heide, Florence Parry and Judith Heide Gilliland. (1990). *The Day of Ahmed's Secret*. Illustrated by Ted Lewin. Lothrop. (P)

Heyer, Marilee. (1986). *The Weaving of a Dream: A Chinese Folktale*. Viking. (I)

Hoban, Lillian. (1981). *Arthur's Funny Money*. Illustrated by author. Harper & Row. (P)

Hodges, Margaret, adapter. (1984). *Saint George and the Dragon*. Illustration by Trina Schart Hyman. Little. (I)

Hogrogian, Nonny. (1971). *One Fine Day*. Illustrated by author. Macmillan. (P)

Howe, James. (1983). *The Celery Stalks at Midnight*. Illustrated by Leslie Morill. Avon. (I)

Huck, Charlotte. (1989). *Princess Furball*. Illustrated by Anita Lobel. Greenwillow. (P,I)

Hurd, Edith. (1972). *Stop! Stop! Stop!* Harper. (B)

Hutchins, Pat. (1971). *Changes, Changes*. Macmillan. (W)

Hutton, Warwick, reteller. (1989). *Theseus and the Minotaur*. Illustrated by reteller. McElderry Books/Macmillan. (I)

Isadora, Rache. (1979). *Ben's Trumpet*. Illustrated by author. Greenwillow. (P)

Juster, Norton. (1961). *The Phantom Toll Booth*. Random. (I)

Keats, Ezra Jack. (1974). *Kitten for a Day*. Watts. (W)

Keats, Ezra Jack. (1962). *The Snowy Day*. Viking. (P)

Kent, Jack. (1975). *The Egg Book*. Macmillan. (W)

Kessler, Leonard. (1966). *Kick, Pass and Run*. Harper. (B)

Kherdian, David. (1979). *The Road from Home: The Story of an Armenian Girl*. Morrow. (I)

Konigsburg, Elaine. (1967). *From the Mixed-up Files of Mrs. Basil E. Frankweiler*. Illustrated by author. Atheneum. (I)

L'Engle, Madeleine. (1980). *A Ring of Endless Light*. Farrar, Straus & Giroux. (I)

Larrick, Nancy. (1988). *Cats*. Philomel. (PO)

Lester, Julius. (1988). *To Be a Slave*. Illustrated by Tom Feelings, Dial. (I)

Lewis, C.S. (1950). *The Lion, the Witch, and the Wardrobe*. Macmillan. (I)

Lionni, Leo. (1988). *Six Crows*. Illustrated by author. Knopf. (P)

Lobel, Arnold. (1970). *Frog and Toad Are Friends*. Illustrated by author. Harper & Row. (B)

Lottridge, Celia Barker, reteller. (1990). *The Name of the Tree*. Illustrated by Ian Wallace. McElderry Books/Macmillan. (P)

Lowrey, Lois. (1989). *Number the Stars*. Houghton Mifflin. (I)

Louie, Ai-Lang. (1982). *Yeh-Shen: A Cinderella Story from China*. Illustrated by Ed Young. Philomel. (P)

Lyon, George Ella. (1990). *Come a Tide*. Illustrated by Stephen Gammell. Orchard Books/Watt. (P)

Mahy, Margaret, reteller. (1990). *The Seven Chinese Brothers*. Illustrated by Jean and Mou-sien Tseng. Scholastic. (P)

Maury, Inez. (1974). *My Mother the Mail Carrier—Mi Mama la Cartera*. Feminist Press. (P)

McCloskey, Robert. (1941). *Make Way for Ducklings*. Illustrated by author. Viking. (P)

McDermott, Gerald. (1974). *Arrow to the Sun: A Pueblo Indian Tale*. Holt. (P)

Mendez, Phil. (1989). *The Black Snowman*. Illustrated by Carole Byard. Scholastic. (P)

Merriam, Eve. (1986). *Fresh Paint*. Macmillan. (PO)

Monjo, Ferdinand. (1970). *The Drinking Gourd*. Illustrated by Fred Brenner. Harper. (P)

Monroe, Jean Guard and Ray A. Williamson. (1987). *They Dance in the Sky: Native American Star Myths*. Illustrated by Edgar Stewart. Houghton Mifflin. (P,I)

Moore, Robin. (1990). *The Bread Sister of Sinking Creek*. Illustrated by author. Lippincott. (I)

Myers, Walter Dean. (1990). *The Mouse Rap*. Illustrated by author. Harper. (I)

Nash, Ogden. (1980). *The Cruise of the Aardvaark*. Illustrated by Quentin Blake. Little. (PO)

Neimark, Anne E. (1986). *One Man's Valor: Leo Baeck and the Holocaust*. Illustrated with photographs. Lodestar. (I)

Norton, Mary. (1953). *The Borrowers*. Harcourt. (I)

Oakley, Graham. (1980). *The Church Mice at Christmas*. Illustrated by author. Atheneum. (P)

O'Brien, Robert. (1971). *Mrs. Frisby and the Rats of NIMH*. Illustrated by Zena Bernstein. Atheneum. (I)

O'Connor, Karen. (1983). *Sally Ride and the New Astronauts*. Watts. (I)

O'Dell, Scott. (1964). *Island of the Blue Dolphins*. Houghton. (I)

Ormerod, Jan. (1981). *Sunshine*. Lothrop. (W)

Parrish, Peggy. (1974). *Dinosaur Time*. Harper. (B)

Parrish, Peggy. (1989). *Good Hunting, Blue Sky*. Illustrated by James Watts. Harper & Row. (B)

Paterson, Katherine. (1977). *Bridge to Terabithia*. Illustrated by Donna Diamond. Harper & Row. (I)

Peters, Lisa Westberg. (1990). *Good Morning, River!* Illustrated by Deborah Kogan Ray. Arcade. (P)

Pitseolak, Peter. (1977). *Peter Pitseolak's Escape from Death*. Edited by Dorothy Eber. Delacort. (I)

Plath, Sylvia. (1976). *The Bed Book*. Illustrated by Emily Arnold McCully. Harper & Row. (PO)

Pomerantz, Charlotte. (1989). *The Chalk Doll*. Illustrated by Fran Lessac. Lippincott. (P)

Prelutsky, Jack. (1988). *Tyrannosaurus Was a Beast*. Greenwillow. (PO)

Price, Susan. (1987). *The Ghost Drum: A Cat's Tale*. Illustrated by author. Farrar, Straus & Giroux. (I)

Rappaport, Doreen. (1988). *The Boston Coffee Party*. Illustrated by Arnold McCuffy. Harper & Row. (B,P)

Reit, Seymour. (1988). *Behind Enemy Lines: The Incredible Story of Emma Edmonds, Civil War Spy*. Harcourt. (I)

Rey, H.J. (1941). *Curious George*. Illustrated by author. Houghton. (P)

Rodda, Emily. (1986). *The Pigs are Flying*. Illustrated by Noela Young. Greenwillow. (I)

Rylant, Cynthia. (1984). *Waiting to Waltz: A Childhood*. Bradbury. (PO)

Scarry, Richard. (1972). *Richard Scarry's Great Big Mystery Book*. Random House. (W)

Schwartz, Alvin. (1982). *There Is a Carrot in My Ear*. Illustrated by Karen Ann Weinhaus. Harper. (B)

Seed, Jenny. (1989). *Ntombi's Song*. Illustrated by Anno Berry. Beacon Press. (P)

Sendak, Maurice. (1963). *Where the Wild Things Are*. Illustrated by author. Harper. (P)

Seuss, Dr. (1957). *Hop on Pop*. Random House. (B)

Seuss, Dr. (1958). *If I Ran the Zoo*. Random House. (B)

Shub, Elizabeth. (1982). *The White Stallion*. Illustrated by Rachel Isadora. Greenwillow. (P)

Silverstein, Shel. (1981). *A Light in the Attic*. Illustrated by author. Harper & Row. (PO)

Simmons, Ellie. (1970). *Family*. McKay. (W)

Speare, Elizabeth George. (1959). *The Witch of Blackbird Pond*. Houghton. (I)

Stanek, Muriel. (1988). *I Speak English for My Mom*. Illustrated by author. Whitman. (P)

Steptoe, John. (1987). *Mufaro's Beautiful Daughters: An African Tale*. Illustrated by author. Lothrop, Lee & Shepard. (I)

Stock, Catherine. (1990). *Armien's Fishing Trip*. Illustrated by author. Morrow. (P)

Stopl, Hans. (1990). *The Golden Bird*. Illustrated by Lydia Postman. Dial. (I)

Strachan, Ian. (1990). *The Flawed Glass*. Little, Brown. (I)

Taylor, Mildred. (1977). *Roll of Thunder, Hear My Cry*. Dial. (I)

Tolkien, J.R.R. (1938). *The Hobbit*. Houghton Mifflin. (I)

Trull, Patti. (1983). *On with My Life*. Putnam. (I)

Turner, Ann. (1989). *Grasshopper Summer*. Macmillan. (I)

VanAllsburg, Chris. (1985). *The Polar Express*. Illustrated by author. Houghton Mifflin. (P,I)

Viorst, Judith. (1982). *If I Were in Charge of the World and Other Worries: Poems for Children and Their Parents*. Illustrated by Lynn Cherry. Atheneum. (PO)

Wetterer, Margaret K. (1990). *Kate Shelley and the Midnight Express*. Illustrated by Karen Ritz. Carolrhoda. (P)

White, E.B. (1952). *Charlotte's Web*. Harper & Row. (I)

White, Ryan and Marie Cunningham. (1991). *Ryan White: My Own Story*. Dial. (I)

Wilder, Laura Ingalls. (1935). *Little House on the Prairie*. Harper. (I)

Wildsmith, Brian. (1980). *Professor Noah's Spaceship*. Oxford. (I)

Williams, Karen Lynn. (1990). *Galimoto*. Illustrated by Catherine Stock. Lothrop, Lee & Shepard. (P)

Williams, Margery. (1970). *The Velveteen Rabbit*. Illustrated by William Nicholson. Doubleday. (P,I)

Worth, Valerie. (1978). *Still More Poems*. Illustrated by Natalie Babbitt. Farrar. (PO)

Xiong, Blia, reteller. (1989). *Nine-in-One Grr! Grr!* Illustrated by Nancy Hom. Adapted by Cathy Spagnoli. Children's Book Press. (P)

Yashima, Taro. (1955). *Crow Boy*. Illustrated by author. Viking. (P,B)

Yep, Laurence. (1989). *The Rainbow People*. Illustrated by David Wiesner. Harper & Row. (I)

Yolen, Jan. (1980). *Commander Toad in Space*. Illustrated by Bruce Degen. Coward-McCann. (P)

Zola, Meguido. (1983). *Karen Kain: Born to Dance*. Franklin Watts. (I)

Zologow, Charlotte. (1972). *William's Doll*. Illustrated by William Rene du Bois. Harper & Row. (P)

Index

T

U

V

W